The Challenge of School Reform

A Journalist's Education in the Classroom

David S. Awbrey

ROWMAN & LITTLEFIELD EDUCATION
A division of
ROWMAN & LITTLEFIELD PUBLISHERS, INC.
Lanham • New York • Toronto • Plymouth, UK

Published by Rowman & Littlefield Education
A division of Rowman & Littlefield Publishers, Inc.
A wholly owned subsidary of The Rowman & Littlefield Publishing Group, Inc.
4501 Forbes Boulevard, Suite 200, Lanham, Maryland 20706
http://www.rowmaneducation.com

Estover Road, Plymouth PL6 7PY, United Kingdom

British Library Cataloguing in Publication Information Available

Library of Congress Cataloging-in-Publication Data

Awbrey, David S.
  The challenge of school reform : a journalist's education in the classroom /
David S. Awbrey.
     p. cm.
  Includes bibliographical references and index.
  ISBN 978-1-60709-713-6 (cloth : alk. paper) — ISBN 978-1-60709-715-0 (electronic)
  1. Middle school teaching—United States—Anecdotes. 2. Awbrey, David S.
3. Journalists—United States. 4. Middle school teachers—United States. 5. Teacher-
student relationships—United States. 6. Teaching—United States. 7. Education—
United States. 8. Educational change—United States. I. Title.
  LB1623.5.A95 2011
  373.1102—dc22

                                                              2010023330

∞ ™ The paper used in this publication meets the minimum requirements of
American National Standard for Information Sciences—Permanence of Paper
for Printed Library Materials, ANSI/NISO Z39.48-1992.

Printed in the United States of America

To my daughter, Grace, and her generation, in hopes that their education
will be as meaningful and their future in the United States
as bright as mine were at their age.

~

Contents

~

CHAPTER ONE

Why Teach? Why Pipkin?

I've spent my life arguing. My mother says that as a child I could coax paint off a wall. For most of my journalism career, I was an opinion writer, commenting on issues ranging from Mideast policy to neighborhood zoning. I've taken on, and held my own against, some of the most powerful people—governors, U.S. senators, corporate CEOs, presidential candidates—in American public life.

But here I am in a seventh-grade social studies class getting verbally slammed by an insufferable thirteen-year-old who is using me as a human piñata before twenty-five other highly amused adolescents.

After more than thirty years working for various newspapers and wire services around the country, I decided to teach history in a lower-income middle school in Springfield, Missouri. Abandoning the cynicism and egoism of journalism, I enrolled at Drury University, a local liberal arts college noted for its education program, received my teaching certificate, and entered the classroom with the idealism and naiveté of a twenty-three-year-old on his first job.

In other words, I was totally unprepared for Marshall Perry.

Marshall was placed on earth to make life miserable for teachers. He was a destroyer of dreams, a dasher of hopes, and a perpetual pest who could sabotage any lesson plan. He was whip-smart—his personality balanced between feral animal and twisted genius. He was obstinately quarrelsome enough to become a cable TV political talk-show host; he was sadistically sly enough to become a serial killer.

A natural agent of chaos, he gave good value for his nastiness. Every day was something different—snapping a girl's bra on Monday, pilfering a neighbor's book on Tuesday, instigating a fight on Wednesday, and so on through the Huck Finn manual of schoolboy mischief. He could quote the Book of Revelation, proof-texting it with the lyrics of Marilyn Manson.

Marshall and I were locked in several primal power struggles: teacher vs. student; adult vs. teenager; old lion vs. upstart cub; authority vs. rebellion; order vs. madness.

I was losing. He knew my disciplinary options were limited to oral reprimands that gave him the opportunity to argue back and banishments to the principal's office that merely reaffirmed his highly prized and well-deserved reputation as the school's reigning bad boy. I also lacked the confident command over kids exhibited by the best veteran teachers. Word spread through Pipkin Middle School: Mr. Awbrey was easy prey. The principal's verdict: Mr. Awbrey has "classroom management issues."

Middle schools demand routine and predictability. Without it, schools would descend into adolescent savagery. That's why administrators spend much of their time prowling the halls and peering through door windows to ensure that students are hunched over their desks, moving their pencils for whatever purpose. My principal practiced the pigeon theory of management—swoop in unexpectedly, poop all over the place, and fly away. I wanted to avoid giving her excuses to enter my classroom—something Marshall was making impossible. He had become an early test of my professional survival.

The occasion came four weeks into the school year, a defining moment when kids decide who is boss. A teacher who fails to assert command faces months of jeering taunts and incessant disruption, making learning impossible. My plan was to humble Marshall during European map study, show that he wasn't as bright as he and everyone else believed, and restore the primeval masculine, hierarchical order in my classroom. I was going to air this punk weasel out.

Marshall sat on the far right side of the front row, where I had quarantined him from the rest of the classroom but could still watch him. Within minutes, he started picking a spat with a neighbor over a notebook. Half-heartedly, really just egging him on, I politely asked him to stop. Body language must have given me away; he backed down when normally he would have responded with brash back talk or profanity.

The air was tense. Marshall's unexpected withdrawal perked the other students up, their internal barometers sensing an ominous disturbance in classroom atmospherics.

Using an overhead projector, I flashed a political map of Europe on the screen to prepare for our upcoming lessons in medieval and Renaissance history. I pointed to various countries whose names had been blanked out and asked the students to identify them. We located Italy, Greece, and Spain. Then came France.

"Isn't it true that all the French are gay?" Marshall growled in a surly, accusatory voice. "Why are we studying a country of homos? That should be illegal. Why are you promoting gays, Mr. Awbrey? Are you gay?"

In middle school, the term *gay* usually refers to anything the kids don't like—pants that aren't blue jeans, almost any book, music favored by baby-boomer teachers. When I gave a test, someone would say "this is so gay" to express their displeasure. This wasn't one of those cases. It was a full-bore assault on me and the authority of teachers in general.

But I welcomed Marshall's challenge and counterattacked head on.

"If you knew anything about France you would see that the gay thing is just a stupid stereotype," I snapped sarcastically. "Furthermore, for your information, I'm married and have an eight-year-old daughter. So, no, I'm not gay."

Sensing an advantage, I pushed ahead, throwing in the classic line from the Jerry Seinfeld show. "Not that there's anything wrong with that."

Huge mistake. I'm not living in Upper West Side Manhattan.

"But Mr. Awbrey, the Bible says that gays will burn in Hell," a normally quiet girl in the corner blurted out in genuine shock that a teacher in the Ozarks of southern Missouri would in any way condone homosexuality.

"Yeh, Mr. Awbrey, don't you know how gays 'do it'? My brother showed me a picture on a fag porn website. It's sick," the class jock chimed in.

Some people will think me a moral coward for not defying such blatant homophobia. They might be right. But in Springfield's pervasively evangelical Christian culture such lessons require that students trust their teacher, a confidence I had not earned in only a few weeks of school.

I retreated. The terrain was strategically hopeless; to them, Marshall held the moral high ground. They thought he had protected the class from a teacher pushing a "gay agenda." I groaned to myself. What would I do when we got to the Italian Renaissance and all those unabashed paintings and statues of shamelessly naked men?

I turned to the screen and pointed. "What's this big country east of France?"

The Road to Pipkin

How did I get here? What crazy notion led me to believe I could teach history to seventh graders, few of whom showed any interest in school except as a place to hang out with their buddies, shove around the weak, gross each other out, shake their booty, eat lunch, and bully anyone who thinks they should act otherwise.

Two years earlier, I left my job as editorial page editor of the *Burlington Free Press* in Vermont because I thought my experiences in politics and public affairs gave me something to offer adolescents who were on the cusp of young adulthood and just beginning to try to make sense of the larger world. Family considerations brought me to Springfield, but I also recognized the city as the perfect laboratory for my secondary motive for entering teaching: to investigate why U.S. public schools are failing large numbers of the country's children.

Nicknamed the "Gateway to the Ozarks," Springfield is home to approximately 150,000 people. While the national news media direct their education reporting mainly toward poverty-stricken inner-city schools or elite private and affluent suburban schools where kids fight tooth-and-claw to gain admission to prestigious colleges, Springfield exemplifies the vast center of the nation's socioeconomic spectrum. It's "God, guns, and NASCAR" America, best known as the headquarters of O'Reilly Auto Parts, Bass Pro Shops, and the Assemblies of God; it's the third largest city in Missouri, the quintessential border state where East meets West and North becomes South.

Similarly, Pipkin typifies education in commonplace America. The student body is 25 percent racial minority. Approximately 72 percent of Pipkin kids receive free or reduced-price lunches, the federal government's primary measurement for poverty, but most of the families of the school's roughly 450 students are best described as working poor or lower middle class, holding minimum-wage or slightly better paying jobs.

Although often marginalized in the nation's education discussions, schools in the country's "flyover" communities like Springfield will largely determine whether the next generation of workaday, grassroots Americans have the academic skills and civic commitment to ensure the nation's future economic prosperity and maintain a thriving democratic system of government.

As a journalist, I covered educational topics in nine states. I watched officials in Pennsylvania decide when to close schools for deer-hunting season, districts in Illinois argue over bilingual education, and the Maryland General Assembly fight about funding inequities between schools in Baltimore and wealthy Montgomery County. I am well versed in the arcana of school finance and the intricacies of educational politics. A handful of the hundreds of editorials and columns I wrote on schooling won major awards.

In addition to conventions of the National Education Association and the American Federation of Teachers, I have attended education-related gatherings sponsored by the National Governors Association, the Education Commission of the States, and the National Conference of State Legislators.

To learn firsthand how education policy was crafted, I even departed journalism and joined "the other side," serving several months as communications director for the Kansas State Department of Education during that state's bitter debate over evolution.

I have followed a generation of fads, theories, methodologies, and other panaceas that promised to improve American education: open classroom, block scheduling, constructivism, cooperative learning, creative thinking, critical thinking, emotional intelligence, multiple intelligences, inquiry-based learning, brain-based learning, multiculturalism, outcomes-based education, portfolio-based assessment, phonics vs. whole language, school-based management, data-based decision making, professional learning communities, school choice, charter and magnet schools, school-to-work movement, school-business partnerships, self-esteem movement, global education, Goals 2000, authentic pedagogy, No Child Left Behind.

Meanwhile, since the 1983 "A Nation at Risk" report warned that U.S. schools were threatened by "a rising tide of mediocrity," I've watched the country pour billions of additional dollars into education, hire thousands of new teachers, increase the percentage of educators with advanced degrees, impose several federal and dozens of state reform plans, mandate assessment exams, and implement scores of "silver bullet" school improvement schemes. Yet all that effort has produced little academic progress.

"Despite resources that are unmatched anywhere in the world, we have let our grades slip, our schools crumble, our teacher quality fall short, and other nations outpace us," President Barack Obama said in a 2009 speech. "We cannot afford to let it continue. What is at stake is nothing less than the American Dream."

I could cite an Everest-sized pile of statistics and reports to underscore the president's point; for brevity's sake I use only one. Results of the 2009 ACT college admission test given to 1.5 million U.S. high school graduates showed that only 23 percent of the students were capable of college-level work, which the testing group defined as a C average or higher in first-year courses in math, English, and science. That statistic is devastating in a society where "college-level skills" are considered indispensable for a middle-class lifestyle.

I had to know why U.S. schools were so inadequate and what might be done to turn things around for the nation's children, especially for the millions of American kids like Pipkin's lower-income students whose opportunity to raise their economic and social status in life hinges heavily on the quality of education they receive.

My first lesson, however, was that the reality of American schooling in-side the classroom is a lot more complicated than what I had written about as a journalist or learned in education school, and that one sociopathic kid can make a mockery of even the best-conceived educational policy or most well-implemented pedagogical strategy.

Order Out of Chaos

Though he was the bane of my existence as a teacher, I genuinely liked Marshall Perry. He had traits that make a good journalist: an instinct for the jugular, a suspicion of authority, and an intuitive awareness that 95 percent of life is bullshit. Lots of potential.

I admired how he had gamed the system. According to literacy tests, Mar-shall read on a twelfth-grade level, making him one of Pipkin's top scorers on the state assessment exams that drive much of public education. He knew the school needed him more than he needed the school.

"Don't worry, Mr. Awbrey," he shouted the first time I sent him to the principal's office for disobedience—for tweaking a girl's breast and wiggling his butt in her face. "I'll be back. They never do anything to me."

Sure enough. His smug, smirking face was there the next day.

Marshall was downright ornery, absolutely incapable of respecting his fel-low classmates or acknowledging that any teacher might have something of value to offer. I could no longer morally tolerate his presence. He was taking class time that should be devoted to attentive students—in effect, he was stealing education from kids with precious few advantages in life.

One day I noticed Marshall wearing a black T-shirt imprinted with the red-circled-A symbol of anarchy.

"So, Marshall," I began, "I assume by your shirt that you are an anarchist. Have you ever heard of the great anarchists like Prince Kropotkin or Emma Goldman?"

For the first time in my class, a trace of uncertainty, of confusion, crept across his face.

"Of course you haven't," I said, honing in for the kill. "That shirt is just a fashion statement. You probably got it at Hot Topic," referring to the punk-rock-themed teen store. "You're a shopping-mall anarchist, a phony, a poseur."

I wasn't trying to disgrace him—well, yes I was, but only to regain some pride and to persuade him that I wasn't the dolt he perceived all teachers to be.

At first-day orientation, a Pipkin colleague said that if I reached one or two kids a year, I would be a successful teacher. I hoped Marshall would be the first trophy to justify my becoming a teacher. After class I apologized if I had embarrassed him and said that if he were truly attracted to anarchy as a political theory, I had some essays he could read about the subject.

He actually seemed interested. Maybe I could get to this kid.

But it wasn't to happen.

Hard to believe, but Marshall acted even worse in his other classes. The administration finally ran out of patience. He was sent to a "behavioral intervention specialist" and was diagnosed with Oppositional Defiance Disorder. They pumped a Woodstock quantity of drugs into him, and he gradually disappeared down the maw of the social service bureaucracy. During all this drama, my suggestion that Marshall was just a teenage jerk pushing everyone's buttons was ignored.

The administration also sent me to an intervention specialist, a veteran teacher who would try to retool my classroom management skills.

Debbie Ponder is the reason I survived Pipkin Middle School to tell this story. My students had become so rowdy that nearby teachers complained they couldn't concentrate because of the clamor from my classroom. At wit's end, I was tempted to take the advice of a student who said I should "whup us like our dads do" to get them to behave.

Mrs. Ponder's method was similar to the "broken window" concept of law enforcement. You sweat the small stuff—tolerate a broken window (low-level crime) and soon the neighborhood is lost. The tiniest infraction draws a megaton response.

I compare Mrs. Ponder to my drill sergeant during Army ROTC boot camp at Fort Benning, Georgia, during the Vietnam War. Total control. Complete command of the situation. No nonsense. No guff. Get to work. Shut up and do as I say. But always in a body-language dialect that said, "I really care about you. This is for your own good."

She silenced chatty Courtney with a glare. She wagged a cautionary finger at Jordan before he could cock his fist to slug a neighbor. She frog-marched wandering Tiffany to her seat. She jolted Sandler awake by smacking his desk with a six-hundred-page textbook. She threatened to transfer moonstruck Britney if the girl did not stop the goo-goo-eye flirtation with her boyfriend across the room.

"They can behave," I realized in amazement as a master teacher went through her paces. "This class doesn't have to be a headbanging mosh pit every day."

To ensure that misconduct bore consequences, I joined other seventh-grade teachers to start a noon detention program. Since lunch is a high point of middle school social life, the possibility of losing chill time with friends was a powerful deterrent. Steadily, things started getting better for me. Maybe this will be okay.

My classroom management troubles stemmed from my inability to make the transition from journalist to teacher. Good journalists pride themselves on ironic detachment. They don't become personally involved. They report and analyze rather than get down and dirty in the muck of life. It's the kind of emotional distance that doctors and police officers develop to cope with the traumas and tragedies they face daily.

To transform myself into a teacher meant I must abandon the journalistic conceit of sideline observer and become an active player. I had to learn to empathize and connect with kids a half-century younger than I and for whom merely arriving at school on time often represented a small act of heroism.

Listening To Their Stories

Under a new district policy, I told the class early in the fall semester, a truant officer would telephone a student's home when the kid was more than fifteen minutes tardy to school. The purpose was to improve attendance to meet mandates of the federal No Child Left Behind law. Sounded reasonable to me—if they aren't in school, children won't learn.

At the end of the period, a visibly agitated girl named Crystal approached my desk. "Mr. Awbrey, can you ask them to not call my house if I'm late for school," she pleaded. "I live with my grandma, and I don't always get to school on time because she sometimes sleeps late and can't bring me. If they call her, she'll get real mad and blame me and hit me."

That's the way it goes in a low-income middle school. Virtually every day, I faced distraught students enduring major crises that I had no ability to solve.

I was immediately taken with Damien, a transfer student from a small town in southeast Missouri. We connected over my classroom poster of Charlie Parker, the famous jazz musician from Kansas City. Like the "Bird," Damien played saxophone. I talked to him about Parker's life and music, how he was influenced by Count Basie and other greats who turned Kansas City into a jazz mecca in the 1930s, and his early death of complications from a lifelong abuse of alcohol and heroin. Often when the class was completing a worksheet assignment, I played a Parker tune and it seemed to help Damien focus. Within a few weeks, however, Pipkin's wannabe "gangsta" element had latched on to Damien. Rather than Charlie Parker, he was all about hip-hop and rap and skipping class and ignoring middle-aged white teachers.

Michael was an exceptionally bright, all-American kid. He was a bench-warmer on the school's basketball team and probably had the most natural intelligence of any boy in the seventh grade. One day, his normal cheerfulness and his desire-to-please-the-teacher were absent. One of his buddies told me the story. Michael lived with his father and cohabitating girlfriend. The woman apparently saw Michael as a rival for dad's affection and issued an ultimatum: either the kid goes or she would. Guess who dad kicked out?

At first I assumed that Kara merely suffered from teenage-morning narcolepsy, which was epidemic among my first-period students. Adolescent brains are not designed for 8 a.m. geography lessons. One day, I tried to rouse her, threatening to send her to the assistant principal's office if she didn't snap to it. Two half-opened groggy eyes looked at me in defiant resignation. "You can't do nothing to me to make my life worse," she groaned. It turned out that Kara's mom was a single parent who worked two jobs, housekeeping at a local motel and waitressing at a Steak 'n Shake diner. Kara was the primary caregiver for two younger siblings. She babysat, cooked meals, cleaned house, laundered clothes, and made sure that everyone got off to school in the morning.

And I'm supposed to teach these kids medieval and Renaissance history?

I wanted to work at Pipkin, thinking I had much to offer kids who had so little. As a journalist I had written extensively on poverty. I had editorialized about the "achievement gap" between affluent and poor kids. I had read think-tank studies on the social ills that afflicted low-income children: poor prenatal care, lack of preschool, inadequate health care, deteriorating neighborhoods, dysfunctional families, bad nutrition, racial and class prejudice, academically deficient schools.

None of that sociology prepared me for kids whose fathers beat them regularly; who stole food from the school lunchroom so their little brother would have dinner that night; who feared that mom's latest live-in boyfriend would sneak into their beds late at night; who were surrounded by filth, stupidity, drug and alcohol abuse, and constant violence; and who worried whether cuts in state Medicaid funding meant they wouldn't get their asthma medication.

And I'm trying to persuade these kids it's important to learn about Charlemagne.

I was furious—at the school system for placing greenhorn, untested teachers like me in the toughest building in the district (more than half of Pipkin's regular classroom teachers had fewer than three years of experience); at a society that scorns the underclass as a parasitic social burden; at the smug, self-important bureaucrats in school administrative offices who blame poor kids for giving the district a bad image because of low scores on state assessment tests. Most of all, I was irate toward myself—for my powerlessness to respond effectively to my students' needs.

Although entering education with what I thought were noble motives and pure intentions, I couldn't become a capable teacher until I got off my big white horse and stopped perceiving myself as savior of the downtrodden poor. I needed to recognize my students not as objects of my own private crusade, my politically correct ego trip to prove I cared, but as children who simply needed someone to trust. I had to meet them at eye level, child to empathetic adult.

Primarily, I had to listen, to treat the students as people with stories to tell rather than empty brains I had to fill with whatever wisdom was contained within the state-mandated social studies curriculum. Gradually—from conversations or casual chats at lunch, in the hallways, before and after class, and in the stands at football games—I got their narratives. Many were heartbreaking. Some were the normal hassles of early adolescence: annoying parents; romantic crackups; hard-grading teachers. I responded as best I could, offering advice, encouragement, or an old bromide from my own father—"Don't let the bastards get you down."

I knew I had made a breakthrough when a girl, saying that some boys had called her this, asked me in strictest confidence: "Mr. Awbrey, what's a douche bag? And am I one?"

It took a bit of tact, but those were easy questions.

Much harder would be to explain to twenty-first-century American teenagers why they should care about people who lived hundreds of years ago on a continent across the Atlantic Ocean.

CHAPTER TWO

~

Imagining History

Mrs. Fairchild was my first history teacher. The great-grandmother of my first best friend, Jackie Simmons, she lived with her family next door to us in Hutchinson, Kansas, in the early 1950s. She had to be well into her nineties. On hot summer days, Jackie and I would sit with her on the front porch of their prairie Victorian house, drink lemonade and snack on cinnamon-laced snickerdoodles while she told stories.

As if entering a movie flashback, she would lower her eyes, catch a train of thought, and pour out tales of a remarkable childhood on the buffalo-roaming plains of the American West.

A young girl in the post–Civil War period, she told of traveling by covered wagon across the Kansas frontier from Fort Hays to Fort Larned, where her father would become the U.S. government Indian agent. The wagon-train master was Wild Bill Hickok, the legendary gunfighter and gambler. "He was the nicest man," she wrote in an unpublished memoir.

Fort Larned was established to protect pioneers journeying along the Santa Fe Trail, and many of Mrs. Fairchild's stories were about Cheyenne, Comanche, and other Native Americans. She recalled her father's advice that when she and her girlfriends rode their horses away from the fort and saw some men in the distance, they should run away as fast as they could if the strangers where white, but not worry if they were Indians. "You could be sure that white men were up to no good," she said.

Amazing. I knew someone who knew Wild Bill Hickok, who would end his days with a bullet in his back holding the "dead man's hand" of aces and eights in a saloon in Deadwood, South Dakota. I ate cookies baked by someone who tossed horseshoes with Indian children and whose babysitters included wives of cavalrymen killed a few years later with General George Custer at the Battle of the Little Bighorn.

Other than family members, no person has affected my life more than Mrs. Fairchild. She taught me never to accept stereotypes of other people. This at a time when Hollywood movies and television Westerns filled screens with savage, untrustworthy Indians conniving to ambush innocent settlers. (Fess Parker's Davy Crockett slaughtering Creeks trying to save their tribal lands was one I particularly remember.) The only good Indian—except perhaps for the Lone Ranger's Tonto—is a dead Indian was the genocidal message promoted to baby boomers.

Since those scorching summer days on Mrs. Fairchild's porch, history to me has never been just facts and dates or lists of kings and presidents, but stories of real people in their unique time and place. The past has become an active part of my psyche. Incredible! Indians once chased buffalo across my childhood front yard.

I wanted to teach students at Pipkin Middle School the lessons Mrs. Fairchild planted in me: Knowledge of history tends to make people tolerant because it helps them respect cultural differences. Human nature never changes. Human motives are inevitably conflicted; the line between self-interest and self-sacrifice is often indecipherable. The noblest intentions may create the worst results. The future is never easier than the past. Regardless how dire the situation, this too shall pass.

Most important, I hoped the kids would develop a historical imagination, an ability to project from the past into the future, to visualize possibilities for their own lives, to place themselves in the lives of others as part of a continuing conversation with those who came before.

Home is where everyone's story begins, so I asked my students to explore their own family tree. I told them to talk to older relatives and learn something about their ancestors. Where did their family originate? What kind of work did their grandparents and great-grandparents do?

Many of the kids got into the assignment. A black student found that an uncle had run a DNA test that traced the family line to a specific tribe in West Africa. A grandfather talked for the first time about being wounded in World War II, earning the respect of his grandson. A few students learned they had Indian blood, quite possible given Springfield's proximity to Oklahoma and its numerous tribes. Could any of them be distantly related to Mrs. Fairchild's girlhood friends?

Several students wondered if stepparents counted—sure, families are more than blood. One girl chortled that her father said she came "from seven generations of white trash." A boy was defiantly proud of a relative hanged for murdering a card shark who cheated him in a poker game. "No one messes with us Jacksons," he boasted.

One of today's perplexing disconnects is that history has never been more popular among the public at large, yet never less emphasized in the typical American school. Such noted historians as David McCullough and Doris Kearns Goodwin have become media darlings with books that routinely top best-seller lists. The History Channel is among the most viewed stations on cable television. Many communities support local history museums and hold annual celebrations to honor their heritage. Sword-and-sorcery-style Renaissance fairs draw eager crowds across the country. Thanks partly to the Internet, genealogy has become a consuming passion for millions of Americans.

Yet large numbers of young Americans remain oblivious to the past, depriving them not only of integral lessons in life but also jeopardizing the future of American democracy. History tests given in 2006 by the National Assessment of Educational Progress, the federal program that measures student achievement, found that 53 percent of high school seniors scored "below basic," which means they were essentially ignorant of anything that happened before last week.

It doesn't get much better in college. A history exam commissioned by the American Council of Trustees and Alumni and taken by seniors at fifty-five top U.S. colleges found that only 19 percent of the students scored a grade of C or above; the average was 54 percent. That so many of America's supposed future leaders know so little history is astounding in a world where long-standing rivalries and resentments often control international relations.

Civilization is not genetic; it has to be learned. If the transmission of a culture's ideals and values breaks for one generation, civilization crumbles and society disintegrates into barbarism. That is especially true in a democracy. What Alexis de Tocqueville called "the habits of the heart"—faith in freedom, trust in people to manage their own affairs, a sense of community—must be constantly renewed and nurtured.

The heart of American democracy is the belief that each individual has worth. My goal at Pipkin was to use history to help students see significance in their experiences—a critical attitude for low-income kids who often feel left out of mainstream America. For example, although she is not mentioned in any history text, Mrs. Fairchild contributed to the transformation of the West. Her life had meaning far beyond her living years.

History teaches young people they are unique—that the story they craft out of their lives will fold into the panorama of human existence. Whether the narrative is well written is irrelevant. It is theirs alone, perhaps to be remembered and treasured as long as the wind sweeps across the prairie like a young girl on an Indian pony.

Sin and the Saint

Humming a little tune, I casually took attendance, strolled to my usual spot at the front of my lectern, and nonchalantly asked this question:

"Who in this class is a virgin?"

Mouths gaped. Faces flushed pink. Heads swiveled around the room.

"Don't answer that," I quickly interjected, chuckling to myself for playing a private joke on them. "I just wanted to be sure you are awake."

To open our lessons in medieval history, I wanted to grab the kids' attention with the topic of sex and sin and St. Augustine, an early father of the Catholic Church and the most influential intellectual of the Middle Ages. Aware that Augustine's religious and philosophical works were beyond the intellectual capabilities of seventh graders, my goal was just to introduce him in the hope that later in their academic careers the name would resonate and lead them to pursue his views in greater depth. I also wished that, once exposed to the impact of his thinking, they would understand that ideas from centuries ago can have consequences today, including notions about the No. 1 interest of teenagers of all generations—sex.

Augustine was born in 354 in North Africa, then part of the decaying Roman Empire. He wrote what is often considered the world's first true autobiography, *Confessions*, in which he laid bare his decadent youth and eventual conversion to Christianity. For more than 1,600 years, his book has been the gold standard for soul-wrenching memoirs of turmoil and redemption; he would have been the perfect guest for *The Oprah Winfrey Show*.

As detailed in *Confessions*, Augustine was a shameless hedonist in his youth, reveling in sexual promiscuity and other forms of vice common in the late Roman Empire. He sired a son out of wedlock and maintained at least two mistresses, much to the consternation of his devoutly Christian mother, Monica. While studying in the northern Italian city of Milan, Augustine began to doubt his pagan beliefs and move toward Christianity. In a famous quote he whined about how difficult it was for him to ditch his libertine lifestyle, praying for God to "grant me chastity and continence, but not yet."

Augustine finally embraced celibacy and helped seal the traditional Christian attitude toward sex, constructing a morality based on abstinence as the ideal and strict fidelity for husbands and wives in marriage. This ethic was a radical departure from the freewheeling sexuality of the Roman Empire and has been part of the Western attitude toward sex ever since.

I pretty much dropped the subject at that point, hoping that the kids might perceive—whether they agreed with him or not—how much influence Augustine still has on twenty-first-century America.

In the spirit of full disclosure, however, readers should know the strong impression Augustine has had on my personal outlook on life and how his ideas permeate much of this book.

Like many cub reporters, I started my journalism career on the police beat, covering cops and courts. I wrote about some of the cruelest actions imaginable by human beings. I remember a man blowing his wife's head off with a shotgun because she flirted with another guy at a bar; their two kids were eyewitnesses to their mother's death. I recall the trial of a drunken driver who killed five members of a family returning home from vacation; the drunk emerged unscathed and never spent any time in prison. I reported about a man pushing a co-worker into a boiling vat of chlorinated cleaning solvent during a job dispute, scalding the victim's body beyond recognition.

Trying to make sense of it all, I was drawn to Augustine's concept of original sin, the theory that there is something inherent in the human condition that tempts us toward sin and leads us to do unconscionable things. I agree with nineteenth-century French writer Joseph de Maistre, who said, echoing Augustine, "I do not know what the heart of a rascal may be; I know what is in the heart of an honest man; it is horrible."

Augustine is also largely credited for Western civilization's conviction that history has purpose and meaning. In contrast, classical pagans construed history as cyclical, constantly repeating itself through the centuries without ultimate significance; bluntly, "life's a bitch and then you die." Augustine interpreted history as linear and under God's control, meaning that positive progress is possible and individuals can affect the course of history.

More to the point of this book, Augustine is among the most important educational theorists in Western history. One of the foremost teachers of his time, Augustine introduced the then-novel opinion that teachers should welcome and encourage questions from students. That attitude helped fashion the inquiring-mind approach to learning that is the hallmark of the Western intellectual tradition. He also urged teachers to apply varying modes of instruction—what today would be called differentiated learning—to meet the unique needs of students.

Augustine's educational ideas stem largely from his doctrine of original sin and its corollary, free will, the belief that humans have the God-given liberty to make up their own minds on any subject and should not be forced to submit to dogmatic authority. Such freedom, however, requires strict intellectual discipline and moral direction to help overcome humanity's tendency toward evil.

For centuries, Augustinian thought underlay formal education and the path to maturity in Western Europe and America. A primary educational goal from the Middle Ages to the twentieth century was to contain the beast within—"In Adam's fall, we sinned all" read the *New England Primer* used by generations of early Americans. By studying admirable role models from the past, young people were to develop strong personal character to master their depraved passions and tame their satanic temptations. To surrender to one's natural inclinations would unleash the hellhounds of greed, lust, egotism, and crime.

Those lessons were taken to heart by American founders—Adams, Madison, Hamilton—who held an Augustinian regard for humanity and created a government of checks and balances to inhibit humankind's intrinsic desire for absolute power.

One of my biggest surprises as I proceeded through teacher training and more deeply explored the mind-set of American education was how thoroughly U.S. schools have abandoned the Augustinian tradition in favor of "child-centered" Progressive educational theories developed in the early twentieth century. Teachers are told to focus on a child's personal development and self-esteem rather than instill intellectual and ethical principles that young minds need to resist evil. Emotional well-being has replaced character building as the central motive of schooling. Education school curricula are dominated by America's therapeutic culture, emphasizing psychology courses designed to enable teachers to release children's natural love of learning impeded as little as possible by adult authority.

Perceiving themselves more as child wellness counselors than sage elders transmitting the wisdom of the past, U.S. educators have jettisoned the intellectual heritage that informed American schools for more than three centuries, helping to create the nation's current existential crisis that is marked by economic uncertainty, cultural confusion, and loss of faith in the future.

Augustine died in 430 as barbarian Vandals were sweeping across North Africa, further accelerating the death throes of the Roman Empire. In upcoming chapters, I will describe how the Middle Ages recovered from this debacle, guided by Augustine's philosophy, in the hope that such ideas might help generate the moral and academic revival so desperately needed today.

Barbarians in Eye Shadow

"What's a goth?" I asked to begin class. "What does it mean to be a goth?"

Several students turned immediately toward Chelsea, who was wearing her everyday look—pageboy-length black hair, raccoon-thick black eyeliner, black nail polish, black-and-gray tartan skirt, red-and-white striped socks with black engineer boots, and a black T-shirt imprinted with the logo of the band Green Day.

Her face frozen in self-indulgent sadness, Chelsea seldom smiled in class, seldom expressed more than disdain for school, her classmates, and life in general. But she had some of the highest grades in the seventh grade, even though she spent considerable class time sketching punk-style fashion designs in her notebook.

"Oh, get off it," she responded to the finger pointing. "You don't know anything. You're so ignorant. This is so lame."

"No, really," I jumped in, seeking to avoid another verbal smackdown or worse among punks, skaters, gangstas, and other Pipkin Middle School tribes. "I'm a clueless old guy. Just tell me. What's a goth?"

"Goths are those weirdoes who hang around Park Central. They hate everyone," one student finally responded.

Chelsea crossed her arms, pursed her scarlet lips, and shook her head in evident disgust.

"So where does the word *goth* come from? Does anyone know?" I asked, trying to get to the point of all this.

Silence, although Chelsea perked up a bit. Curious perhaps?

The Goths, I explained, originated in Scandinavia and were among the barbarian hordes that demolished the Roman Empire in the fourth and fifth centuries. In the Renaissance, the term became a catchall to brand anything medieval as rude or unsophisticated. The current use stems from the nineteenth century's fascination with death and the macabre surreal, as found in gothic novels by Mary Shelley, Edgar Allan Poe, and Bram Stoker, creator of the Count Dracula tales. Jim Morrison, the Lizard King and heroin-overdosed lead singer of the rock group The Doors, partly inspired the goth revival in the 1970s.

So goths descend from a long historical line, I said, tying marauding, bearskin-wearing Germans pillaging ancient Rome to *The Rocky Horror Picture Show*, Anne Rice's vampire books, and the *Twilight* series.

To show that history is relevant—if only as a borrowed label for one of today's teenage clans—the goth reference was intended to link the past to today's teen world.

I noted that the fall of Rome in the late 400s began the medieval period, a word derived from the type of Latin spoken during that time. "So what does anyone know about the Middle Ages?" I asked, attempting to ascertain how much the kids had been exposed to the era they would spend the next few months studying.

Some giggled. Some shrugged. Several slumped in their seats and made fake snoring noises. Most just sat motionless, hiding themselves in the crowd.

"Weeell," I stammered, stalling as I realized that this might be a problem. "How about King Arthur? Knights in shining armor? Ladies in white linen? Cathedrals? Crusades? Dungeons and dragons?"

Saved, a hand. "Wasn't that movie *Braveheart* about the Middle Ages?"

"Dude, that was great. Whack. Whack," a kid shouted out, swinging his arms in an air-guitar rendition of a sword fight.

Since knowledge builds on knowledge, I pressed ahead to understand what background the students had in the medieval period. "Did you have any of this in elementary school?"

Blank stares. A few incoherent mutterings.

"I think there was something about the Vikings in fifth grade," Isaiah finally volunteered.

Toss out the lesson plans. This is not good. More than 1,200 years of history in three months: the creation of the nations of Europe; the establishment of the university; the spread of Christianity; the roots of representative democracy; art, literature, music, philosophy, and much more that have shaped Western moral values, religious beliefs, and cultural institutions. These students knew none of it, aside from Mel Gibson's blue-body-paint biopic about a legendary Scottish warlord.

Like any panicked teacher, I sought refuge in the textbook.

"Turn to page 106 in your books and, Jessica, could you begin reading the section on the recovery of Europe after the barbarian invasions."

Jessica and several others read about how the Franks, Goths, and other barbarian tribes calmed down after ransacking the Roman Empire and how Charlemagne gradually restored order in Western Europe, culminating with this section from the book:

Charlemagne brought the rule of law to a large area of what had been the Western Roman Empire. He also supported the Catholic Church. In return for this support, Pope Leo III crowned Charlemagne emperor on Christmas Day in 800.

"What does this mean?" I asked. "What's going on in what you just read?"

Collectively, their eyes looked away from me—to the floor, the ceiling, the walls, their desks, anywhere but toward the front of the room.

"Don't you understand what the text said?" I pleaded.

A hand rose tentatively, sheepishly.

"What's a pope?" she asked.

"Good question," I said, grateful for any reaction. "He's the head of the Roman Catholic Church—like Pope John Paul II."

"What's the Western Roman Empire?"

"The area that in the Middle Ages encompassed today's Western Europe, countries like Germany, France, Spain, Italy, and England."

"The Roman Catholic Church—is it Christian?"

This didn't make sense. How could kids go through seven years of formal education and pick up nothing about medieval European history except "something about the Vikings"?

The answer came from a veteran social studies teacher.

"They don't take much history until middle school."

Mind-boggling, but true. Neither the Springfield Public Schools nor the Missouri Department of Elementary and Secondary Education requires history from kindergarten through third grade. They get a once-a-week smattering of Missouri history in fourth grade—a bit on Daniel Boone, a mention of Lewis and Clark, a nod to the Civil War, a passing reference or two to Mark Twain and Harry Truman. In fifth grade, they get a brief introduction to the European discovery of America—"something about the Vikings"—and a perfunctory overview of early U.S. history.

In the sixth grade, they finally study ancient Mediterranean societies, which along with the Middle Ages and Renaissance in seventh grade are the only times—K–12—that Springfield students encounter those three critically important periods of Western history. Asian, African, and Latin American history are scarcely touched.

Springfield is no different from hundreds of American school districts in forsaking a globally inclusive and sequential study of history during a child's most formative years. Much of it stems from federally mandated standardized tests that concentrate on math and reading skills. In Springfield, as in many other U.S. communities, if a subject isn't on the state test, it gets the short shrift. No wonder U.S. students score miserably on history tests. They seldom study history; they never learn it in the first place.

My anger intensified as I realized that this neglect of history in the early grades is especially damaging to low-income children like my students at Pipkin Middle School. These kids don't have the opportunity to travel, books at home, college-educated parents, and other resources that enable middle-class students to compensate for a liberal-arts-depleted elementary school curriculum.

For many of my students, I was their last chance. If they didn't acquire an appetite for history in middle school, they probably never would, an incalculable loss to them and to a society that depends on citizens conversant enough with the past to move confidently and wisely into the future.

~

CHAPTER THREE

Teaching Charlemagne

As Xavier walked by an eighth grader in the crowded hall, the older kid bumped him. Xavier, who reminded me of a Latino version of the cocky but loveable delinquent played by Mickey Rooney in the movie *Boys Town*, reflexively shoved the guy against the lockers lining the wall.

"Xavier," I cried out. "Get over here. Come on. What are you doing? He didn't mean anything. It was an accident. Now go apologize. Do the right thing."

I was serving as the between-periods hallway monitor, so I couldn't let the incident slide. As part of the district's "character education" program, the school was trying to reduce the level of animosity and anger the kids displayed toward one another, encourage them to show mutual respect, and behave in a civil manner.

But Xavier would have none of it.

"You don't understand, Mr. Awbrey, around here, if you apologize for something like that, it's a sign of weakness. Now, that guy leaves me alone. He's more careful in how he acts around me. He knows I'm no pansy. I apologize and everyone is after me."

I couldn't argue with the logic. Street cred is everything in a low-income middle school. A smallish kid like Xavier would be a tempting target for bullies were he not willing to retaliate forcefully to any perceived sign of disrespect.

In many ways, middle school, regardless of economic class, resembles a wild dog pack, especially among the boys. Each kid is finding his place in the hierarchy—with alpha status going to the toughest, most aggressive adolescent, the one most able to assert his own will over the rest of the group.

Watching this brutal Darwinian drama every day, I often thought of William Golding's 1954 novel, *Lord of the Flies*, which depicts a group of middle-school-aged adolescents marooned on a desert island who quickly devolve to primal barbarism—to what seventeeth-century English philosopher Thomas Hobbes called "nature red in tooth and claw."

The theme of Golding's book is the conflicting tendencies within all humans between civilized stability and lawless liberty. The young castaways form tribes that compete for dominance; the struggle ends in murder and bloodlust for more violence. Children, who a short time before were well-mannered English choirboys, descend into complete anarchy, until order is restored by a British naval officer who rescues the kids from their own evil impulses.

The incident with Xavier occurred while I was teaching the fall of the Roman Empire. I couldn't help notice that in both the concrete-floored halls of Pipkin Middle School and the marble-columned Forum of the doomed "eternal city," the thin veneer of civilization was under constant attack. Although it's intellectually suspect to draw parallels too closely between very different historical eras and circumstances, some worrisome similarities are noteworthy between ancient Rome and contemporary America.

For more than 1,500 years, historians have debated the demise of the Roman Empire. The consensus is that the collapse was due largely to centuries of internal societal rot that made Rome vulnerable to barbarian invaders eager for plunder and conquest.

As the fifth-century social critic Salvian analyzed it, the destruction of Rome was the consequence of economic exploitation, political corruption, and licentious debauchery. The empire, Salvian said, had sunk into "a slew of immorality rarely known in history; adultery and drunkenness are fashionable vices, virtue and temperance are the butts of a thousand jokes."

You don't have to be a pinched-nose moralist, only a casual observer, to recognize disturbing resemblances between Salvian's Rome and contemporary America, as exemplified by Wall Street, the U.S. Congress, and Hollywood.

Kids sense it. Visit any public secondary school and the effects of today's culture are evident in young people who are exceptionally vulnerable to the larger messages of society: insatiable greed, political opportunism, and moral cynicism. I don't want to belabor what is apparent to anyone who watches television or movies, listens to popular music, or follows current affairs, but we are sacrificing a generation to a celebrity-worshipping, wealth-driven, egocentric ethos that delights in trashing the traditional qualities of hard work, education, and common decency.

As scores of nations and empires have learned to their misfortune, no society is guaranteed its survival. Continued success comes only when the young are baptized in the positive core values and principles that undergird civilization. Sadly, such time-forged truths are lost on the vast numbers of young Americans today who detect little that is noble or uplifting in much of modern U.S. society.

But history always offers hope. While the fate of the Roman Empire should be a cautionary tale for twenty-first-century America, the rebuilding of Western society by Charles the Great—in French, Charlemagne—during Europe's darkest age provides a beacon to light our own perilous way to the future. Charlemagne's example teaches contemporary Americans that education is critical to the political and cultural growth of society. His eighth-century schools educated substantial numbers of literate people who organized a stable government, generated new wealth, and flowered spiritually and artistically. Certainly, we in twenty-first-century America could learn much from people who pulled Europe out of brute stupidity and revived Western civilization.

A Warrior's Curriculum

The most extraordinary story I covered while a reporter for United Press International was the arrival of the first female midshipmen at the U.S. Naval Academy in July 1976.

The young women—girls really—were not welcomed with salutary canon blasts, to say the least, at the previously all-male military school on the shores of the Severn River in Annapolis, Maryland.

While the eighty-one teenaged female plebes lined up in their freshly cut military-bob haircuts and pristine Navy whites for Induction Day ceremonies in front of Bancroft Hall, where they would billet under the same roof with their male classmates for the next four years, resistance against women middies reflected the changes they meant to the nation's military traditions.

Using their saltiest seadog language, the critics unloaded: How dare these women think they are qualified to command the country's naval and marine forces? This is women's lib run amok. These gals are a danger to national security. They can't hack it; just watch them drop like flies during Plebe Summer. They aren't allowed in combat; why should they get into Annapolis? They are taking the place of men who should have been admitted.

In my UPI news dispatch of the event, I quoted a retired admiral who, I thought, captured the attitude of many old and young sailors: "These women will never fit into the 'warrior culture' of the Navy and Marine Corps."

Over the past three decades, female service academy graduates and other women in the armed forces have shown incredible courage fighting sexual harassment and gender bigotry from some of their male colleagues. They have performed with consummate professionalism on the battlefields of the Middle East. They have risen to the top ranks of leadership in all branches of the military. Only people with strong military qualities could survive such tests, so critics had no need to worry about any deterioration of the nation's "warrior culture" because of these women.

I told that anecdote about women at Annapolis to my seventh graders for two reasons. The first was to connect with students from military families. Most were proud whenever I mentioned their relatives' contribution to national defense, and I tried to find every reason to do so. I asked Sylvie, whose mother was a U.S. Army helicopter mechanic in Iraq, whether gender made a difference in the military. "Women can't do some stuff, like infantry, but my mom likes it . . . not the being away but doing something important."

I was surrounded by children of America's warriors, who are drawn largely from the Pipkin stratum of society. Pipkin teachers were delighted when a former student enlisted in the armed forces. It meant the kid had made some good choices in life; the U.S. Army doesn't recruit losers. For the neighborhood, the military represents upward mobility at a time of limited opportunity. Fortunately, Pipkin had been spared any military deaths, but when, for example, a student showed me a photo of her dad with the dusty mountains of Afghanistan looming in the background, the school became one of the few places since 9/11 where I felt the country was truly at war.

The second reason for the female warriors of Annapolis story was to teach the inescapable historical lesson that an element of a "warrior culture" is incumbent for civilization. As Yale historian Robert Kagan observed, war is "the default state of the human species." The Roman Empire discovered too late that without people skilled in battle and willing to risk their lives for their fellow citizens, no civilized society can survive the ever-present dangers of barbarism.

Charlemagne could be viewed as the medieval prototype for that American military icon, the officer and gentleman/woman—the commander educated in the arts of war and the arts of cultured living. For himself and his warrior elite, Charlemagne revived classical learning as the best training for leadership. Updated for the eighteenth century, a similar traditional curriculum molded many U.S. founders—freedom fighters who modeled themselves after Cincinnatus, Fabius, Scipio, and others in the citizen/soldier/farmer/ statesman tradition of the Roman Republic.

When Charlemagne became king of the Franks in the late eighth century, Western Europe was a rural cultural backwater where people lived in extreme poverty under constant threat of famine, terrorized by wandering bands of thuggish barbarians. Life expectancy was no more than thirty years, and medical treatment consisted primarily of folk remedies and magical incantations. The magnificent Roman aqueducts and roads lay in disrepair; people wandered about the ruins of once-splendid ancient cities unable to read the inscriptions on the crumbling buildings.

For the future of Western civilization, Charlemagne's foremost accomplishment was to launch an educational reform movement by ordering his bishops and abbots to establish schools in their cathedrals and monasteries. Under the guidance of an English monk named Alcuin, these schools nurtured the Carolingian Renaissance, a brief moment when arts and literature flourished amid the general ignorance and squalor of the age. Among its accomplishments was the Carolingian minuscule, lowercase letters still in use today, a major typological advance over Roman writing that used only uppercase letters.

Ordering schools to "make no difference between the sons of serfs and of freemen, so that they might come and sit on the same benches to study," Charlemagne created the West's first system of universal public education—something not replicated until Horace Mann in early nineteenth-century New England.

The curriculum in Charlemagne's schools was based on the classical seven liberal arts, an academic framework that can be traced to Greek philosophers Plato and Pythagoras and was later influenced by Augustine. Younger students studied the *trivium*: grammar, which focused on literature; rhetoric, which centered on history; and dialectic, which dealt with philosophy. Older students continued with the *quadrivium*: arithmetic, which included analysis of numbers; geometry, which covered geography and surveying; music, both performance and theory; and astronomy, which contained physics and advanced mathematics.

Variations of this core curriculum were standard in Western education for centuries and still prevail in many European and elite American schools. Most U.S. public schools, however, have discarded such intellectual rigor in favor of Progressive educational theories. That development is a primary reason why, as regards literacy and quality of mind, today's American students lag far behind earlier generations.

Education's Cultural Illiterates

When I was in college, the academic keystone at the University of Kansas was the Western Civilization program. Modeled after the Great Books curricula at Columbia University and the University of Chicago, the two-semester class required students to read some of the seminal works of Western culture—"from Beowulf to Virginia Woolf"—followed by discussion groups and capped off with a written exam.

Created shortly after World War II, the program was intended to expose college students to the foundational ideas and values of Western civilization that had been mortally threatened by Nazi totalitarianism. The approach was reminiscent of the revival of the liberal arts by Charlemagne and Alcuin in the early Middle Ages as a barricade against barbarism.

Western Civ was required for graduation from KU, but in the late 1960s the school of education exempted its students from the comprehensive test. Apparently too many education majors were flunking the exam; besides, education professors argued, studying the principal concepts of Western thought wasn't paramount for teachers. They mainly needed to know how to teach, not what to teach; any good teacher can teach any subject with the right (Progressive) strategies.

The only unique aspect to the decision by KU education professors to jettison the Western Civ test was that they still required their students to have at least a passing acquaintance with the sustaining texts of Western society. Most of their colleagues in other education colleges had long before dismissed the liberal arts as peripheral in educating teachers.

"By temperament they [education professors] have no interest in learning or capacity for it; by purpose they are bent not on instruction but social work. They care little about history or science or good English," Columbia University historian Jacques Barzun wrote in his essay, "The Art of Making Teachers."

Underscoring Barzun's comments, huge numbers of teachers have graduated from KU and other colleges without knowing much about history, literature, philosophy, or similar subjects once considered the seal of an educated person. Many of the very people responsible for transmitting to schoolchildren the salient tenets of Western civilization—the intellectual wellsprings of American democracy—are illiterate in their own cultural heritage.

Few of today's educators have the scholarly credentials that would qualify them to teach in a medieval school. Not only did prospective teachers in the Middle Ages study the liberal arts of the *trivium* and *quadrivium* for six or more years to win the laurel wreath symbolic of a bachelor of arts degree, they spent an additional year to earn a master's degree that was a license to teach.

Aspiring medieval teachers were also among the best students of their generation because education was among the most respected professions of their time. That's a far cry from today, when teacher candidates tend to be among the least academically inclined students and attend the least prestigious colleges.

A study by Michael Kirst, an education professor at Stanford, found that compared to students in other disciplines "education students have low grades and dismal SAT and GRE scores," noting that aspiring teachers ranked fourteen out of sixteen occupational groupings on SAT verbal and fifteen out of sixteen on math scores.

"Schools of education are cash cows to universities," said Edwin J. Delattre, former dean of the Boston University School of Education. "They admit and graduate students who have low levels of intellectual accomplishment, and these people are in turn visited on schoolchildren. They are well-intentioned, decent, nice people who by and large don't know what they are doing."

My experiences at Drury University confirmed these criticisms. Although most of my education school classmates were fairly intelligent, few were motivated scholars. The most common reason I heard for why they wanted to teach was that they "loved children." No doubt enjoying the company of kids is important for a teacher; however, it would have been reassuring had the teacher trainees also expressed strong interest in their academic discipline, especially on the secondary level. None ever did. Nor were they encouraged to do so, being told repeatedly by Progressive education professors that "teachers should teach children, not subjects."

Education colleges make it difficult for would-be teachers to become familiar with a broad continuum of knowledge or immerse themselves in serious scholarship. Since the education coursework for a teaching certificate usually requires roughly two years to finish, most teachers—and most education professors and school administrators—have barely more than freshman/sophomore-level exposure to subjects outside education. (When I pointed out how little academically substantive coursework teachers had in college, a superintendent in Kansas told me, "It's sad that we expect people to sacrifice their own education to teach.")

Much of that effort is wasted. It apparently makes no difference in student performance whether a teacher has an education degree or takes another route to the classroom. A 2009 study commissioned by the U.S. Department of Education found no correlation between teacher effectiveness and teacher-training coursework. It also seems to make no difference on student achievement whether a teacher has a master's degree in education or not.

Common sense suggests, however, that teachers who combine strong subject knowledge with extensive hands-on training in pedagogy will be more likely than graduates from other programs to manage their classrooms well and have the intellectual acumen to engage students in learning. That's how some of the world's best school systems educate their teachers.

Finland, a top scorer in international academic comparisons, is one of the best models. Like other high-performing countries, such as Canada, Singapore, and South Korea, Finland recruits teachers from the top ranks of its college graduates. Finnish teachers must have a master's degree in their subject area, in addition to education courses, and once in the classroom they have real power over curricula and other school policies. Contrary to the low status of American teachers, Finnish teachers enjoy the same social esteem as doctors and lawyers.

A template that might work well in the United States is remarkably similar to the medieval apprentice system. A college graduate with a major in the liberal arts or similar substantive subject who wants to teach spends a year shadowing a master teacher during the day while taking education courses in the evening. This "residency model" recognizes that most teachers learn their craft by emulating veteran colleagues—a mentor who takes yearlings under her wing and shows them how to manage a classroom and reach young minds. Such a structure could dramatically upgrade instruction.

Several factors give the United States a chance to transform the teaching profession. The baby-boom generation is entering retirement, creating a demand for new teachers. Some of these teachers could come from the ranks of highly talented, well-educated professionals displaced during the recession of the past few years. The economic troubles also could encourage liberal arts and other subject majors to consider a teaching career, which might not offer a large salary but has compensating attractions in job security and personal satisfaction.

America needs teachers who can connect the younger generation to the great ideas and deeds of civilization—who can offer children role models from history and literature to counter the rapacious investment bankers, conniving politicians, and misbehaving celebrities who dominate contemporary culture. If we don't get such teachers, a twenty-first century rewriting of *Lord of the Flies* will be a documentary of our children's lives.

CHAPTER FOUR

~

A Monk's Education

At 3:15 a.m. a bell rings to summon the monks at Assumption Abbey to worship. About a dozen men dressed in floor-length white robes file into a spare, wood-paneled chapel to begin their day of prayer, work, and meditation on a remote hilltop in the Missouri Ozarks.

Members of the Cistercian Order of the Strict Observance—also known as the Trappists—follow a 1,500-year-old way of life dramatically at odds with the values and priorities of contemporary America.

Established in France during a church reform movement in the late eleventh century, the Cistercian monks live according to the *Rule for Monasteries* laid out by St. Benedict of Nursia in the early sixth century. Like their predecessors, the monks at Assumption Abbey take vows of chastity, poverty, and obedience. They live communally in a low-slung, sprawling, blond brick-and-cinderblock complex that looks something like an American elementary school from the 1960s.

Established in 1950 near Ava, Missouri, the monastery initially tried to support itself through farming, but that proved unprofitable in the thin, rocky soil of the Ozarks. They then turned to handmade concrete bricks, until a lower-cost competitor drove them out of that business. Finally, upon advice of fellow monks in Kentucky, they began baking rum-soaked fruitcakes that are sold through the Internet and the Williams-Sonoma catalog. Annually producing roughly 25,000 fruitcakes targeted at the Christmas market, the enterprise enables the monks to maintain their monastery financially and provide for charitable giving while allowing them time to study, pray, and counsel a steady stream of visitors and spiritual seekers who often stay at the sparsely furnished guest house.

As I clicked through photographs of Assumption Abbey on the classroom LED projector, I hoped my seventh graders would become intrigued by an alternative lifestyle far removed from televisions and iPods, rock stars and lame-brained celebrities that dominate popular culture. Rather than the helter-skelter pandemonium of Pipkin Middle School, Assumption Abbey offered a life of strict discipline and clockwork regularity—a rigid schedule of seven daily prayer sessions, reflective silence, and dutiful labor for the good of the community. Yet there also was a timelessness to the place that collapsed centuries of tradition into a living historical moment, a medieval remnant tucked into the ancient hills of southern Missouri.

Although I knew of the Cistercian Order from the books of Thomas Merton, a Trappist monk and one of the most popular religious writers of the twentieth century, I had never truly appreciated the serene appeal of the monastic life before visiting Assumption Abbey. I hoped through our discussion of monasticism in the Middle Ages that my students would likewise realize, however vaguely, that life has more options than those promoted by the entertainment media and that history offers role models who will never appear on the cover of *People* magazine.

By this time—roughly two months into the academic year—my classroom management skills had improved enough to keep my head above water on most days, though adolescent havoc always churned just below the surface. The greater control permitted me to focus less on my own pedagogical shortcomings and more on understanding middle school kids.

I was especially troubled that the students had little curiosity about anything other than their own lives and surroundings. They lived outside history; they had no interest in how the past shaped their personalities and mind-sets. They had no sense of themselves as unique individuals. At an age when young people should be forming their own identities and figuring out where they fit into the world, they instead defined themselves according to mass-marketed images and products promoted on television—reinforced by pitiless peer pressure that demands conformity in everything from clothing styles to moral values.

Contrasted to the spiritual contentment of the Assumption Abbey monks, my students were afflicted with the joylessness of shriveled souls. True self-awareness is impossible without large blocks of solitude—ample time for study, reflection, and self-examination that leads to a vibrant inner life. And time for themselves is what today's kids don't have or seem to want. A huge percentage of their waking hours is consumed by outside influences—especially various forms of electronic media—to the point that many kids don't have even a second to daydream. They no longer control their own imaginations.

When Charlemagne resurrected Western civilization from the chaotic centuries that followed the fracturing of the Roman Empire, monasteries were pivotal to his education program because monks were among the few literate people in early medieval society.

Almost every medieval monastery had a *scriptorium*, or writing room, where monks would painstakingly transcribe ancient manuscripts. These anonymous copyists preserved much of the classical learning we have today, building a literary Noah's Ark of the formative texts of Plato's Greece and Cicero's Rome.

Monks were also the primary teachers of the Middle Ages. It's estimated that 90 percent of literate medieval Europeans learned to read at monastic schools.

That heritage is again at risk of being lost. At no time since ruthless Vikings rampaged across Europe in the decades following the death of Charlemagne and destroyed much of his civilizing educational work has reading been as endangered as it is today in the United States.

That's an astonishing claim, but one fully supported by recent studies and test scores showing a drastic decline in the reading abilities of young Americans. According to international comparisons of reading achievement, American children are falling behind peers in other countries in basic literacy. For example, on the 2007 Progress in International Reading Literacy test, ten countries or jurisdictions, including Hong Kong and three Canadian provinces, scored better than the United States. In 2001, only three countries were ahead of the United States.

The most troubling fact about literacy in the United States is that the longer American children stay in school the worse they perform compared to foreigners. In the third and fourth grades, U.S. kids do fairly well versus other developed countries; by eighth grade they have drifted steeply downward.

The American reading crisis was further confirmed in a 2007 study by the National Endowment for the Arts that found the same deterioration in reading from elementary to middle school. Dana Gioia, NEA chair at the time of the report, suggested several causes for the drop in reading abilities, including the proliferation of digital and other electronic devices and the failure of schools to inculcate reading habits. Added Gioia, "We live in a society where the media does not recognize, celebrate or discuss reading, literature and authors."

Centuries ago monks lifted Europe out of the swamp of ignorance and illiteracy. Maybe they can help today. Perhaps as they go about their daily schedule of work and worship, the monks at Assumption Abbey can say a prayer for American children.

Misreading Strategy

If you are like me, you can read every word of this paragraph but understand nothing except that it apparently concerns a sports event.

> Four balls later, Anderson extracted the prize scalp of Tillakaratne Dilshan, Sri Lanka's centurion against South Africa, who had been frustrated for 11 probing deliveries in which his only scoring shot was a prod down to third man. He fell to a scything slash to point off the fullest delivery of Anderson's spell, whereupon Mahela Jayawardene was pinned for 9 as he attempted an over-ambitious flick across the line.

The piece is from a British newspaper account of a cricket match. All I know about cricket is that it is sort of like baseball and players use a flat-sided bat to hit a ball; therefore, I can't follow the action the reporter describes. Reading the story, however, reminded me how my seventh graders responded to their early lessons in medieval history.

We were doing group reading about monasticism—passages like:

> In the writing studio of every monastery, the brothers dipped their sharpened quills into their vials of colored acid and continued copying the ancient manuscripts.

A girl named Randi read the section perfectly, neither mispronouncing nor stumbling over a single word.

"What's going on? What are the monks doing?" I asked her.

"Some guys are copying something with some kind of thingy," she replied.

I was baffled. Randi read superbly but comprehended little of what she read. Like me and the cricket report, she didn't get it. The passage didn't make sense. She didn't know the relevant details.

The axiom in education is that children first learn to read and then read to learn. Somehow, many of my middle-school students seemed to have missed that fundamental transition, which usually begins around fourth grade.

Several days later, my suspicions were confirmed. Early in the school year, the students took the Scholastic Reading Inventory, a computerized test designed to assess a child's reading abilities. I was aghast at the results: a few kids were chart-busters with high-school skills, but a huge number fell well beneath literacy expectations for seventh graders, many as low as third grade.

I immediately realized that, while my subject was social studies, I was also going to teach reading; otherwise, the students would never grasp history, a discipline heavily dependent on the ability to absorb a wide variety of information.

Although it meant recasting my course outline, I was okay with teaching reading. Given the unique nuances of history—or any other subject—teachers well versed in content should help students know how to tackle the material.

I needed advice, however, and appealed to the school's literacy coach, who agreed to give me a quick lesson on reading instruction. Wheeling a cartful of basic readers into my classroom, she ran the kids through a battery of reading strategies.

She had them "identify the main idea" and "make judgments" on the selections. They were told to classify, draw conclusions, make inferences, sound out difficult words or phrases, pose questions about the passage, and identify the author's purpose. The kids worked the assignment like expert craftsmen—circling, underlining, boxing—until their pages resembled a blur of symbols and words demonstrating a complex formula in advanced physics.

When I asked why the kids weren't reading history texts as part of their lesson but instead were poring over such fairly vacuous selections as a teenager learning to drive or an animal raising its offspring, I was told that the operating theory in American education is that reading is a transferrable skill.

That is, once kids can decode—translate printed marks into sounds and sounds into words—they can apply that ability to any kind of literature. By deconstructing a narrative about, say, camping in the Ozarks, a child would gain literacy competence to help comprehend other writing, whether descriptions of the creation of the universe or histories of the reign of Charlemagne. The more adeptly the student applied all-purpose reading strategies, the better she would read.

Over the next few days, I photocopied sections from our history text and had the students employ the reading strategies on them. It was obvious that the kids were quite familiar with such exercises, having been drilled in them since early elementary grades. Yet the same fundamental problem remained: They couldn't give a coherent explanation of what they had read. They were especially stumped over basic facts—for example, geography ("Where is England?"); time frames ("Did Charlemagne live before or after Rome fell?"); social class ("Are aristocrats higher than peasants?"); politics ("Is a king the same as a president?").

The literacy coach insisted it would shake out. If I just kept pushing the strategies, the kids would soon be reading medieval history as easily as cell phone text messages. I doubted it.

I turned to the twenty-first century know-it-all: Google. Typing in "how to teach reading," I encountered the name E. D. Hirsch Jr., an English professor at the University of Virginia and respected scholar of language who had much to say about reading.

Eureka! I found the answer.

Author of such books as *Cultural Literacy: What Every American Needs to Know*, *The Schools We Need and Why We Don't Have Them*, and *The Knowledge Deficit*, Hirsch is one of the most important figures in national school reform. Not surprisingly, given his opposition to much of the Progressive ideology that is conventional wisdom in education colleges, his name was never mentioned during my training to become a teacher.

Hirsch promotes the outrageous—to the educational establishment—notion that facts and content matter in education, especially in learning to read. While insisting that decoding, phonics, and other literacy tools are requisite, Hirsch adds that full comprehension hinges on subject-specific "domain knowledge." That idea challenges the "process" theory prevailing in most U.S. schools that command of the written word requires little beyond a firm grasp of literacy mechanics.

Noting the woeful performance of American children on literacy tests, particularly in upper grades, Hirsch wrote in *The Knowledge Deficit*, "I believe that this indifference to specific, cumulative subject matter, more than any other single trait of reading programs, has prevented them from significantly improving reading comprehension."

It clicked. My students didn't understand their textbook because they encountered almost no history when learning to read. Illogically, while elementary schools spend countless hours on reading strategies, they ignore subject matter—the background knowledge—that is intrinsic to true literacy.

To heighten the absurdity, many schools complain that pressure to improve reading skills under the No Child Left Behind law forced them to deemphasize social studies, science, arts, and other content-rich subjects to make more room for the very reading programs that have failed so miserably. Nonsensically, educators have killed the cure to their own disease.

According to Daniel Willingham, a psychologist at the University of Virginia, Hirsch's approach is supported by research in cognitive psychology and psycholinguistics.

"The mainspring of comprehension is prior knowledge—the stuff readers already know that enables them to create understanding as they read," Willingham wrote in the *Washington Post*. "What happens if the reader doesn't have the prior knowledge the writer assumed she had? The reader will be confused and comprehension will break down."

Bingo! An exact description of many of my students—weak readers, but not their fault, because the textbook publisher thought they knew things their elementary school had never taught.

That insight also made me feel better about one of my own literacy gaps. As an American, I was culturally deprived of cricket; no wonder I couldn't comprehend "an over-ambitious flick across the line."

Recovering the Core

Thanks to a donation from a local philanthropist, about one hundred copies of USA Today were delivered every morning to Pipkin Middle School. Briefly reliving my boyhood career as a carrier for my father's newspaper, I would grab a dozen copies to drop off in the teachers' lounge or put in my classroom for students. I seldom got any takers at either place. The rest of the papers, stacked on a table in the school lobby, were usually dumped in the recycling bin, unread.

I declared Fridays newspaper day in my class. I divided the students into four groups, each taking a section of USA Today. After reading their section, they were to list the top three stories and report to the rest of the class.

I wanted students to see the daily newspaper as a rough version of history's next chapter. By realizing that the twenty-first-century conflict between the West and Islamic extremism is partly rooted in the twelfth-century Crusades, for example, they might recognize that the Middle Ages still impact current affairs. Or by reading about politics, they might learn to appreciate the link between U.S. democracy and the Magna Carta, which forced England's King John to cede some power to his nobles in 1215.

A former journalist, I was aware of surveys showing that the younger generation had not acquired the newspaper habit, but I was unsettled by the reaction to the USA Today assignment.

"I hate newspapers," one boy asserted. "My grandmother is the only person I know who reads them."

"I don't just hate newspapers," another boy declared. "I hate reading."

Not only did they resist reading USA Today's general news and business sections, they didn't like the pop culture, celebrity-deifying Life section, and not even the athletes cared for the sports pages. "I can see it on ESPN's Sports Center," a Pipkin basketball player said. "I don't need to read about it."

That reaction is not encouraging for Americans who believe that democracy depends on a well-informed public. And don't say members of the younger generation are getting serious news from the Internet. They aren't. A 2007 study by Harvard University's Shorenstein Center found that most teenagers don't pay much attention to news, period. Instead, their nonschool hours are devoured by television, YouTube, Facebook, video games, pop music, fashion or celebrity and other teen-targeted websites.

Schools deserve much of the blame for this indifference to public affairs. The depreciation of knowledge-based curricula in the schools, especially the study of history and civics, means that the United States is losing its common culture, the social unity that comes from citizens sharing a coherent ethical and intellectual framework. The old idea that schools are training grounds for democracy—that there are certain philosophical assumptions, basic concepts, and documents that all literate Americans must know to enable them to engage in constructive dialogue—is rapidly disappearing. Disconnected from the nation's traditions and formative values, unaware of the lessons from the country's past and its democratic heritage, today's young people could well lack a thoughtful commitment to America's unique historical role to advance freedom and human dignity once they become the nation's leaders.

Western civilization has been here before, when it had to find a path toward recreating itself or risk falling into an abyss of ignorance and cultural despair.

As noted earlier, after the death of Charlemagne in 814, Western Europe was on the precipice. On one side, it was under attack by a newly emergent, militant Islam that had moved aggressively out of Arabia, swept over North Africa, controlled most of the Mediterranean Sea, conquered Spain, and threatened France and Italy. From another direction, waves of marauding, seaborne Norsemen sailed from Scandinavia, plundering England and Northern France and reaching as far as the Volga River in Russia and the islands of the Mediterranean.

The flickering flame of Western civilization was kept alive by small bands of monks in monasteries throughout Europe. These monks salvaged the works of the classical age; transmitted reading, writing, and elements of learning to succeeding generations; and maintained a semblance of social order through their disciplined lifestyle and loyalty to the church. Their efforts preserved the academic and moral resources to enable Europe to gradually rebuild itself.

Through their failure to adopt a solid K–12 curriculum based on the liberal arts and sciences, American educators have begun to rupture the intellectual tradition that undergirds Western culture. Remember, it takes only one generation for a society to lose its collective memory and for barbarism to return. In a world beset by brutal antidemocratic and anti-American forces, the failure to educate an informed and perceptive U.S. electorate could be catastrophic.

Hope is not lost. In recent years, several prominent school reformers have advocated a return to a solid curriculum that would expose young Americans to the history, literature, and ideas that shaped the modern world.

Foremost among them is E. D. Hirsch, the University of Virginia English professor cited previously on lagging American reading skills. Hirsch first gained national attention through his best-selling 1987 book, *Cultural Literacy*, which argued that a common body of knowledge is one of the key elements holding a society together. Hirsch also developed a model curriculum stressing the traditional liberal arts and sciences that is now used in some schools around the country, many of them in low-income neighborhoods where children often lack the cultural and academic advantages of wealthier peers.

Similarly, a group of reformers created an organization in 2008 called Common Core to encourage schools to adopt curricula concentrated on the arts, foreign languages, history, literature, and science to ensure that U.S. children received a well-rounded education. "Of course children must know how to read and compute, but children must be knowledgeable in addition to being skilled," said Lynne Munson, Common Core's executive director and a former deputy chair of the National Endowment for the Humanities. Too many American kids, she added in an interview with *Education Week*, are getting "an incomplete education."

One thousand years ago, at the start of the eleventh century, Europe was slowly regaining its cultural confidence. The Muslim threat had receded. The Vikings were settling down in Normandy and other parts of Europe. Learning was expanding, and the foundations were being laid for the great universities that would transform the continent's intellectual life. Monasteries were flourishing, and their monks would lead a churchwide reform movement designed to end corruption and other abuses of authority and install a better-educated clergy.

That cultural revival, whose roots have renewed Western civilization since the eleventh century, was possible only because European monks during the previous dark years continued to educate the younger generations and conserve the intellectual capital of the classical era.

Let's hope that, while they don't need to wear monks' robes, today's core curriculum advocates can create a similar cultural renewal in this generation.

CHAPTER FIVE

~

Generation Global

When the veteran teacher peeped into my classroom, this is what she saw.

I'm standing in front of a large map of Europe with a pointer aimed at various countries whose names have been blanked out. As I tap a particular country, students enthusiastically raise their hand to identify the nation and its capital. If they miss, they can call on any classmate for the answer. The game keeps the kids bouncy, eager to show off their knowledge in front of their buddies.

"Belgium," a student calls out, then stammers over the capital.

"A green vegetable . . ." I prompt.

"Sprouts City—Brussels," several students shout, repeating a memory phrase we had used previously.

Frustrated by my students' weak background in history because their elementary schools barely—and poorly—taught the subject, I vowed to fill some major knowledge gaps, starting with European geography. After all, how can a kid figure out medieval Britain without being aware of the English Channel?

Meanwhile, I was appalled that the U.S. educational system, in an increasingly international society, disparages simple geography—finding countries on a map. Although members of the first truly global generation of Americans, most of my students had reached seventh grade without knowing the location of France, Brazil, China, and other important countries, or even what continents they are on. In response, I went old school, asking them to color and label maps; memorize national borders and capitals; and identify rivers, seas, plateaus, mountain ranges, and other significant physical features.

Later that day, the teacher who had looked into my classroom caught me in the hall. "Mr. Awbrey," she began, "as a new teacher, you might not realize this, but your instruction I observed this morning is incorrect. What you are doing is nothing more than rote learning, drill-and-kill that discourages authentic learning."

I gave her a noncommittal smile, not wanting to antagonize someone who could ruin me with the principal.

"You see, Mr. Awbrey," she continued, in a condescending education-doctorate voice. "The kiddos can find map facts on Google or use a GPS. You must understand, we are trying to teach them critical-thinking, problem-solving, and learning-to-learn skills. Memorization wastes time. Besides, they so love technology; we must use it whenever we can."

I politely thanked her for the advice, which confirmed my belief that many of the theories that dominate contemporary education are profoundly misguided. In this case, as a former journalist who frequently wrote about foreign affairs, I knew that a mental map of the world was obligatory in a global society. If young Americans don't realize, for example, that Jerusalem is less than one thousand miles by nuclear-armed missile from Tehran, they won't understand a principal geopolitical factor that could dramatically affect humanity's future.

Worse, setting up a false conflict between factual knowledge and higher-order thinking contradicts common sense. How can you think insightfully or solve problems without knowing the specific details and nuances of an issue?

Yet, instead of solid academic content, educators have stressed abstract learning processes, consigning "mere facts" to the keystrokes of a web search. In his book, *The Schools We Need and Why We Don't Have Them*, E. D. Hirsch wrote that my experience was typical for U.S. schools: "The scarcity of memorization is hardly surprising. A vigorous attack on rote learning has dominated education schools, professional journals and teachers' lounges for many decades."

Especially bizarre, this aggressive antifact crusade waged by many educators goes against Bloom's Taxonomy, the revered classification system that teachers are encouraged to use when drafting lesson plans, tests, and other learning strategies. Published in 1956 by Benjamin Bloom, a University of Chicago education professor, the taxonomy—often depicted as a pyramid—creates a hierarchy of thinking, from knowledge at the base to analysis and evaluation at the top. Teachers are supposed to shepherd students up the ladder of learning, mastering each step and integrating the various objectives along the way.

Bloom's Taxonomy makes complete sense to me, a former YMCA swimming coach and journalist who spent much of my early career covering college and professional sports. Getting the fundamentals down is the prescription for proficiency in any discipline, whether swimming, geography, or violin. Repetition—practicing flip turns, memorizing national capitals, or running musical scales—enhances learning and expertise; it doesn't kill them.

Moreover, my students loved map instruction. They were seldom more engaged in class than during Daily Geo, a lesson borrowed from another teacher in which I listed five geography-based questions—"What is the capital of Peru?"—and had them find the answers in their student atlases. Watching them, I recalled my childhood delight thumbing through atlases: the blotches of color distinguishing the countries, the evaporating red as the British Empire shrunk during the post–World War II decades, the meandering blue rivers tracing the course of trade and settlement, the mountains soaring out of green and tan plains through gradually darker brown heights to whitecapped peaks.

I could only wish such simple pleasures for my students, but it would never happen if I accepted the antiknowledge creed prevailing in most U.S. public schools.

I didn't. I kept going with my round-the-world map memory exercises.

And I felt vindicated. At the end of one especially raucous map game, a student who hadn't done well had a request.

"Mr. Awbrey, can I borrow an atlas to take home and look at tonight?"

The World Won't Wait

The challenge Americans face to compete against Asian economies crystallized in my mind when a Chinese acquaintance described his country's primary advantage against the United States: "You Americans don't understand how hard we are willing to work and how little we need for ourselves."

"What he is saying," I told my middle-school students, "is that the information age has leveled the playing field. You are growing up at a time when education—what's called 'intellectual capital'—will largely determine how successful America as a nation and you personally will be."

I was in tent-revival sermon mode. I pleaded passionately for the students to understand how the digital revolution and all that comes with it are transforming virtually every aspect of life in the twenty-first century—that their moment in history, the era they will live in, is being shaped by each click of a computer mouse in ways no one can possibly predict.

My background as a journalist and history fanatic, I hoped, would give me standing as someone who recognizes long-range trends. Perhaps the students would perceive that school could prepare them for a global reality that will crush any slackers. "You've got to be serious about education," I scolded them, "because half a world away kids your age are studying night and day to beat you in an unforgiving world marketplace."

Blank stares and affectless faces told me what they were thinking. "Yeh, yeh. Blah, blah, blah. So what? Why does he drone on about this? Boooring . . ."

Like Cassandra prophesying the Trojan horse, I feared gaining nothing but the bittersweet satisfaction of knowing that I had forewarned them against disaster.

Pressing on, I showed a PowerPoint outlining how severely the United States is falling behind global rivals. An updated version would include these items:

- America's post–World War II educational advantage has eroded as a greater percentage of students in more and more countries graduate from high school and college and score higher on achievement tests than students in the United States, the Organization for Economic Cooperation and Development reported in 2010. Fewer than 70 percent of U.S. high school students earn a diploma.
- In a 2009 study, "The Economic Impact of the Achievement Gap in American Schools," the McKinsey organization, a global consulting firm, tracked U.S. and foreign students through their school years and concluded that "the longer American children are in school, the worse they perform compared to their international peers."

As I plowed through the PowerPoint, I became increasingly exasperated. I was galled that the students do not give a hoot about their own schooling. They seemed unable to connect their apathy—or, for some, active hostility—toward education to the fate that awaits them in a few years. Unless they come around quickly, they will join the millions of other low-income kids who leave high school with no skills and no plan of what they want to do with their lives.

But I was even madder at an educational establishment and a society that had allowed this to happen. India and China aren't to blame. We are the ones turning so many young Americans into dysfunctional citizens, incapable of participating effectively in the nation's democratic system, providing a decent quality of life for themselves, or maintaining America's economic power.

"Our educational failure is the largest contributing factor to the decline of the American worker's global competitiveness," Todd Martin, a prominent international investor, told *New York Times* columnist Thomas L. Friedman.

Confronted with impassive indifference among students and petulant denial by many educators toward problems in American schools, I nonetheless generated a bit of optimism out of my childhood memories of another global crisis that led to major reforms in education.

When I was in fourth grade in 1957, the Soviet Union launched *Sputnik*, the first satellite to orbit Earth. The event sent the United States into a nationwide panic. The Russians had beaten us into space. They had the technical skill to threaten this nation's survival. The United States could lose the Cold War.

Deciding that schools were an integral element in its defense strategy, the United States made an unprecedented effort to improve education. Shades of my own harangue fifty years later, I remember my elementary teacher saying that school was our battlefield "to fight the Russians," who were depicted as faceless automatons who studied constantly—including Saturday!—on orders from a despotic government dedicated to America's destruction.

Meanwhile, in 1958, Congress approved the National Defense Education Act to enhance science, math, and foreign-language instruction in U.S. schools and colleges. Several of my older sister's high-school classmates were able to attend college and become teachers thanks to NDEA grants.

It worked. Schools upgraded curricula and teaching, and the country expanded college access, helping make the baby boomers the best-educated generation in human history. To cap it off, the United States landed a man on the moon in 1969, confirming American scientific prowess and stimulating decades of technological innovation that contributed greatly to the ultimate collapse of the Soviet empire.

That educational edge has been squandered. According to the National Center for Public Policy and Higher Education, a larger percentage of Americans aged thirty-five to sixty-four have college degrees than those aged twenty-five to thirty-four. Today's young adults are the first generation in U.S. history to be less educated than their parents, at a time when much of the world is surpassing America's children in the classroom.

Too many Americans think that global supremacy and a high standard of living are God-given entitlements. They aren't. Neither the future nor the world will wait for the United States to get its schoolhouses in order.

Consuming Capitalism

Rebecca made a horrible fashion mistake one autumn day, and it almost destroyed her reputation. She wore a sweatshirt with the label "Hollister" emblazoned across the front.

"Preppy! She's a preppy," a classmate shouted when he saw her. "Rebecca is a preppy. She probably shops at the Gap with all the snobs."

"Do not," she retorted, realizing that her clothing choice had broken the uncompromising, student-dictated dress code. "I'm no preppy. I got it at a yard sale."

Next to being called gay, nothing was more cutting at Pipkin than to be called a preppy, which in a low-income middle school reeked of status seeking and elitism. Hollister, J. Crew, Abercrombie & Fitch, and similar high-dollar teen brands were for the spoiled brats living in the McMansions on the south side of Springfield, not the poor kids in the gritty neighborhoods on the north end of town.

That doesn't mean that Pipkin students weren't fully plugged into the teenage consumer culture. Teachers spent much of their day confiscating cell phones, iPods, and other classroom disruptors, must-have merchandise for contemporary adolescents. The class-conscious fashion rules, however, were mercilessly policed. Any deviation from the gender-neutral Pipkin "uniform" of scruffy jeans; trendy sneakers; heavy metal, goth-punk, or sports team T-shirt and grungy hoodie was cause for social exclusion and vicious mockery.

Seizing a teaching moment, I asked the kids where their clothes were made. They glanced at the tags: Vietnam, Honduras, Bangladesh—"wherever that is," a kid said with a shrug of his shoulders.

"It's in South Asia, next to India," I responded. "But your stuff comes from all over the world, right? This is another example that you are a global generation. The shirt on your back and the jeans covering your butt come from somewhere else."

"And that brings us back to the Middle Ages."

By now, I could connect almost anything to the medieval era. The students would think they had me wasting class time chasing down a rabbit hole—another journalism anecdote, perhaps, or some current events story—but I had learned to wind my way back to the original lesson more quickly. This time I wanted to link the American teen economy to the world's original international trading system.

I pulled down the world map to chart centuries-old trade routes.

Consider a fourteenth-century lacquer box from China that I saw in a London antiquities store. How did it get to England? It might have traveled by caravan on the Silk Road across Central Asia to a port in Palestine or Syria. From there, the item could have been carried in an Italian ship across the Mediterranean to Venice. It then could have been taken across the Alps to the Rhine River and sent north, possibly to Bruges, the wealthy Flemish trading city. At Bruges, the box was perhaps sold to an English wool merchant who took it home as a gift for his wife.

In that scenario, the foundations of modern global capitalism can be seen. A hypothetical French entrepreneur, perhaps tapping into a European consumer market fascinated by Marco Polo's famous visit to the court of Kublai Khan in the thirteenth century, haggled with an Arab trader in the Middle East for the lacquer box, jade carvings, silks, and other Chinese exports. The venture might have been financed by a loan from German bankers or by Dutch investors who bought shares—a part of the profits—in the merchant's cargo. The English buyer might have paid for his box with a florin, a gold coin minted in the Italian city of Florence.

Substitute sweatshirts and sneakers for the lacquer box and it is essentially the same global economy we live in today.

And why are so many American kids wearing sweatshirts manufactured in Bangladesh and other poor, third-world countries? Because of what economists call "the law of comparative advantage"—countries that produce goods the most efficiently and at the lowest cost will get the work and jobs that come with it.

That brought me to another constant theme: that young people must have massive amounts of education. No American, I explained, can survive sewing sweatshirts for $5 per day, but to millions of people elsewhere in the world five bucks is a decent wage. That requires young Americans to have high-level skills lacking in underdeveloped nations to maintain their accustomed standard of living.

Ironically, the same financial forces that have flooded suburban malls and inner-city discount stores with low-cost foreign products are damaging the future prospects of American children.

In recent years, marketers have identified a new category of consumers— "tweeners," generally defined as kids between the ages of nine and fourteen. This group is a roughly $250-billion-a-year market for everything from lip gloss to Mac laptops. They are part of a consumerist youth culture devoted to getting and spending. Most kids, regardless of social class, fully embrace the commercial ethic aggressively marketed in teen-targeted advertising and other media. It's a closed loop of consumption and entertainment that overwhelms attempts by teachers and parents to encourage kids to see life beyond the next hot item or hip style.

While the economic slump of the past few years might have reduced the volume and price of teen purchasing, it's doubtful that the underlying materialism has significantly changed. The children don't recognize any options—intellectual or spiritual—to perceive themselves other than by how they look and what they own.

And that's why Rebecca never wore her Hollister shirt to school again.

The Future of Our Past

My most successful attempt at edutainment—amusing the students while hoping they actually learn something—was the Time Traveler.

Wearing the pink conical cap from my daughter's fairy-princess Halloween costume and the black robe from my wife's doctoral degree regalia, I entered the classroom dressed like a wacky magician amid the soundtrack of the *Also Sprach Zarathustra* theme music from *2001*, Stanley Kubrick's futuristic movie.

I explained that I was a voyager from the twenty-third century sent two hundred years back in time to collect materials for a museum exhibit called "The American Teenager in the Early 21st Century." My character wanted to talk to Pipkin Middle School students to get first-person reports of their lifestyle and collect cultural artifacts to represent their history.

"What should I put in this museum," I asked the students, "to show your great-great-great-great-great grandchildren how you lived?"

The kids quickly picked up the spirit of the moment: Compact discs. Video recorders. Television sets. Sports paraphernalia. T-shirts. Backpacks. Sneakers. And so on through much of the detritus of contemporary adolescence.

As they named various items, I looked quizzical. "I have seen images of these things in our history logs, but we aren't sure how to use them. How do you operate a cell phone? We know it's a primitive communication device."

A kid pulled a phone from his back pocket and played along, demonstrating text messaging and other features.

My patronizing response: "A clever, if quite primitive combination of printed and spoken word. Of course, we don't need such things. Mental telepathy was perfected in the middle of the 22nd century. We have a nanophotonic circuit in our brains to connect our thoughts with another person's mind."

This went on for fifteen minutes or so. I explained that in the future food was no longer grown or raised on farms; we simply swallowed pills that provided all our vital nutrients. They talked about teenage tastes in music and clothes. I mentioned genetic advances that enabled parents to select the skin tone, eye color, gender, height, and other traits of their children, who were conceived in test tubes and gestated in incubators to eliminate the hassles of sex and pregnancy.

My purpose was to get the kids to see themselves and their society through the eyes of others—a critical element of self-awareness. I also hoped that talking to a person from an imagined future would help students learn to evaluate a past society on its terms, not perceive it simply as an early prototype, a beta version of our own culture.

If students, for example, recognize that their state-of-the art cell phones will one day be antique-store curiosities, they might be less susceptible to what British writer C. S. Lewis called "the snobbery of chronology"—thinking ourselves superior to our ancestors because we have more advanced technology. Instead, we might recognize our common condition with people long dead—that all humans face life challenges—and perhaps wonder whether we will respond to them as well as our forebears did decades or centuries ago.

I also sought to use history to help this global generation of children understand other societies. Reciting one of my favorite quotations, the opening line of twentieth-century British author L. P. Hartley's novel, *The Go-Between*, "The past is a different country; they do things differently there," I told the students that the ability to detach themselves from the tyranny of the immediate is an intellectual skill that could give them intimate access to cultures of all ages.

To reinforce those teaching goals and complement the Time Traveler's field trip to the past, I took the students on a visual tour of teen life in the Middle Ages. I made transparencies for the overhead projector from drawings in a child's coloring book of the workaday medieval world.

I showed pictures of medieval children in typical tasks, tending goats and geese, fetching water for horses, gathering fruit, and churning butter. Another drawing was a row of students sitting on a bench at a cathedral school while a monk read to them from a book mounted on a lectern. I displayed images of older children working as household servants or apprentices learning such crafts as carpentry, weaving, winemaking, or blacksmithing. But it wasn't a life of chores only. Medieval society enjoyed numerous religious holidays, when young men would stage wrestling or archery matches amid the pageantry of whatever saint's day or church event was being commemorated. Annual fairs brought traveling merchants—selling everything from iron pots to Asian spices—and entertainers, jugglers, actors, and dancers to the community.

Their diets rich in whole grains, fruits, and vegetables, with pork, fish, and rabbit providing animal protein, medieval people ate more healthily than do most modern Americans. Sugar was rare and costly, so medieval teeth were generally cavity free. Predictably adolescent, the seventh graders got a huge kick out of a picture of young men drinking beer, the most popular beverage of the era.

I wanted my students to identify with these portraits of children from long ago, to recognize themselves as heirs to centuries of human activity that can enrich and broaden their own life possibilities. As the most multicultural generation since the Middle Ages, the more today's kids can sense the delight a medieval girl had chasing a goose down a country lane, the better prepared they are to reside in the global village and feel comfortable around the endless varieties of human experience.

CHAPTER SIX

~

Class Matters

"Who wants to be rich?" I asked the students.

Hands reached for the ceiling. Heads perked up. High fives were exchanged.

"YES!!!"

"Well, you're lucky you came to school today," I continued, "because I'm going to pass on advice from one of the wealthiest men in the world—a guy named Warren Buffett."

As I explained to the class, when I worked as an editorial writer for the *Omaha World-Herald* in the mid-1980s, Buffett was a member of the paper's board of directors, and I had a chance to chat with him during a lunch with other staff members.

The famed "Oracle of Omaha," perhaps the most brilliant financial mind of his generation, gave us his now-familiar stock-picking advice: Buy low, sell high. Look for solid companies with good long-term prospects—companies you would personally own if you had the money.

The lesson in basic Buffett was prompted by a survey I took a few days earlier. I asked the kids the usual stuff—hobbies, favorite foods, what they did in their spare time. I also asked them about career goals.

Although no one expects seventh graders to have well-drawn life plans, I was disconcerted by how many said they wanted to become professional basketball players, fashion models, or winners on *American Idol*—even though they had no discernible talent or physical attributes for any of those goals.

Several boys said they intended to emulate Springfield native Brad Pitt and become a movie star and link up with a "hot babe" like Jennifer Aniston or Angelina Jolie.

Early adolescence is a wonderful time for impossible dreams, but I wanted to slip in a dose of reality.

I flashed that day's stock tables on the screen and explained how people buy shares in companies—pointing to Disney, Burger King, and other teen-favored businesses—and if things go well they receive part of the firm's earnings as dividends or sell the stock at a profit when its price increases.

Where do you get the bucks, the green, the jack, the coin, the capital to invest?

From working and saving. And to get a good job, you need a good education.

I listed the top employers in Springfield: health care; federal, state, and local governments; public schools and local colleges; Chase Credit Card Services; Kraft Foods; and retail sales, including the corporate headquarters of Bass Pro Shops and O'Reilly Auto Parts.

Most of those jobs, especially the better paying non-Wal-Mart ones, demand at least a high school education and some advanced training or college.

I wanted the kids to think about the future, something difficult to imagine when you come from a family where life is consumed by day-to-day struggles to pay the rent and buy groceries. For many of my students, the lunch menu posted daily outside the school cafeteria constituted long-range planning.

I cited statistics linking higher incomes with higher levels of education. I did the math on how difficult it was to survive on a low-paying job: A person with a $10-an-hour job will earn around $1,600 a month. A decent two-bedroom apartment in Springfield will cost $450 a month; utilities run about $100; food another $100 to $200; add in taxes, clothing, health insurance (if available), a television, stereo, furniture, entertainment, and a car and you were quickly under water financially.

"You mean I can get a car?" one kid responded. "That's what I want."

"You know, Mr. Awbrey, you can eat a lot more cheaply than you say with the dollar value menu at McDonald's," said another.

"Go to the Victory Mission and you can get lots of stuff for free," a voice of experience replied.

Trying to regain control, I cited experts who say that three things are key to avoiding poverty: graduate from high school, don't have children before age twenty-one, and don't have children unless you are married.

"But my cousin is fifteen and she has twins and she's doing fine," came a rebuttal.

My brief economics lesson taught me that a primary difference between lower-income and middle-class students is that poor kids don't have a "future story" to live out. They can't connect what they should do today with what is required to succeed tomorrow. They don't see school as relevant because education is premised on the need to prepare yourself to achieve future goals. Their family narrative is one of continual crisis, a constant struggle to find gas for the car or diapers for the baby rather than to prepare for college or pursue a career.

The year before, I student taught at Springfield's Cherokee Middle School, a self-regarding sanctuary of middle- and upper-middle-class privilege, pastel polo shirts, and Guess jeans. A comparison:

Pipkin is 25 percent racial minority; Cherokee is 7 percent nonwhite. Seventy-two percent of Pipkin students receive free or reduced-price lunches; 14 percent do so at Cherokee. Forty percent of Pipkin seventh graders scored proficient or above on the 2007 state assessment test; 74 percent of Cherokee students met grade-level expectations.

This "achievement gap" is not just economic or academic. It is profoundly cultural. When I taught the Renaissance at Cherokee and showed photos of the Sistine Chapel in the Vatican, a girl had seen Michelangelo's masterful ceiling paintings based on the Book of Genesis while on family vacation to Rome. She brought in pictures and talked about the experience. Her classmates listened closely, as if plotting their own trip to Italy.

At Pipkin, the response to the same lesson was far different:

"Italy? Rome? Vatican? Where are they at?"

"Why should I care about some sissy-friss chapel? It sounds so gay."

"I don't like Italian food, except pizza."

"Is that what God and Adam really looked like?"

Buy low, sell high. It sounds so simple.

The Parent Gap

"Did you see how cracked and rotten her teeth were, and that scraggly yellowish hair? She's got to be a meth addict," Stephanie Beaty said.

"And did you catch the blurry tattoos on the guy—father? boyfriend? . . . whatever he was." I responded. "That was 'prison ink'—someone used a ballpoint pen to make them. Wonder what he was in for."

Mrs. Beaty taught science on our seventh-grade team so we had the same students in class. That conversation came during a break in parent-teacher conferences, which revealed a lot about our students and their family backgrounds. The sessions provided another window into the culture of poverty that enveloped the lives of many of our kids.

Approximately eighty-five students were members of the seventh-grade Blue team. Our leader, a veteran math teacher, had notified every family about the annual conferences. Fewer than half replied that they would attend; the parents of about twenty-five kids ultimately showed up.

The turnout was discouraging, but not surprising. Although we scheduled meetings for afternoon and evening, low-income parents have many legitimate excuses for missing school gatherings—work demands, child care needs, transportation issues. But many don't make it for other reasons—apathy, forgetfulness, dislike of teachers based on their own school experiences, reluctance to hear more bad news about their kid's grades or behavior.

Since the child usually attended the conferences, an unofficial protocol prevailed. Teachers didn't trash the student, fearing that any criticism might lead to a whipping or other punishment once the kid got home. Instead, while noting room for improvement in various areas, we always found reason for praise: "Courtney always participates in class discussion," which was code for "the girl is a chatterbox who won't shut up." Or, "Sam is one of the most entertaining boys in school," which in teacher-speak meant "your son is the class clown whose antics distract everyone from schoolwork."

The kids were active co-conspirators in avoiding parental confrontation, playing their part by nodding their head knowingly and smiling mockingly at whatever lame anecdote a teacher told about them.

"You sure we're talking about the same boy? Because at home he's just one potty-mouthed little smartass," a bewildered parent asked when we described a complete stranger as her son.

Parent-teacher conferences reveal that the "achievement gap" between affluent and low-income children is as much a chasm in family upbringing as in scores on standardized tests.

At affluent Cherokee Middle School, you couldn't keep parents away from meeting the teacher. Most came mainly to be congratulated on being terrific parents, to be told that their children were admirable young scholars, perfectly behaved, and that they had better keep saving for medical or law school. Sometimes, however, the "helicopter" style of parenting backfired: One kid admitted his weak academic performance was vengeance against an overbearing father who never stopped ragging him about his grades or marginal athletic abilities.

"The most consistent predictors of children's academic achievement and social adjustment are parent expectations of the child's academic attainment and satisfaction with their child's education at school," concluded a survey of research on student success conducted by the Michigan Department of Education.

That seems obvious. Yet some people believe that a teacher who spends about an hour a day with a kid in a class of twenty-five to thirty other students will have more influence than parents who have been with the child since birth.

And where the family fits in the nation's socioeconomic hierarchy largely shapes parental attitudes toward schools.

Middle- and upper-class parents have the skills and resources to directly affect their child's education; they know how the system works and can direct it toward their kid's best interests. Even the most concerned low-income parents, in contrast, are often intimidated by schools and teachers, lack political clout to change school policies to benefit their kids, and don't have the intellectual confidence or knowledge to help their children with academics.

Affluent parents are more likely than poor parents to monitor homework and limit television time, to talk about college and careers, to be on guard against smoking, drug abuse, and sexual experimentation. And wealthier families have the financial ability to seek professional help—a good tutor, therapist, or lawyer—to remediate any academic deficiency, self-destructive behavior, or juvenile delinquency. One mistake can ruin a poor kid for a lifetime.

Schools usually mirror their students' social class. Pipkin always hovered on the edge of bedlam. Any spark—a skater dissing a gangsta—could set off a hallway melee; a fire drill could ignite a free-for-all. Cherokee was orderly, businesslike. Pipkin kids often resisted being in school; many of them didn't think it was worth their time. Cherokee children were personally invested in school, realizing that it had a direct bearing on their future. Misbehavior was an accepted form of amusement at Pipkin; at Cherokee monkey business was a sign of gross immaturity.

American educators tend to be uncomfortable about class. Though they prize the ideal of diversity, they typically limit the category to race, ethnicity, or gender, seldom applying it to obvious economic disparities. They are especially reticent when class is linked to personal behavior and family dynamics.

Approximately 38 percent of babies born in the United States have single mothers, most of them teenagers or low-income women. The out-of-wedlock birth rate among Hispanics is 50 percent; among African Americans it is 71 percent.

Children growing up in single-parent households are at increased financial, psychological, and academic risk. Children without involved fathers are more likely to commit crime and abuse drugs and alcohol. Single-parent children have more health problems and lower cognitive skills than children from two-parent families.

In an American society ever more segregated by class, schools are one of the few places where the classes mix—not among students, who are separated by neighborhood real-estate values, but between middle-class teachers and poor students. Social tension was always present, and it gave me insights unavailable had I taught at Cherokee or another affluent school.

Poor kids might lack the cultural literacy that comes with a middle-class childhood, but many of them compensated with a show-me skepticism that forced me to prove the value of medieval and Renaissance history. That meant I couldn't just toss out an assignment and have it completed the next day. I had to use art, literature, music, and other forms of learning to engage them in the subject. I searched for memorable stories and compelling personalities from the Middle Ages to overcome their habitual attitude that anything schoolwork-related must be worthless and boring.

Above all, I hoped—despite my own severe doubts—the American promise that education could transform young lives was still true; that, unlike in other countries and historical eras, my students' futures were not determined primarily by circumstances of birth and social class.

"Anyone can get knocked down," I said repeatedly. "What makes a difference is whether you get up."

Inspiring words? Perhaps. But even while saying them, I knew they weren't necessarily true.

Civil Rights Education

Charles F. McAfee did the unthinkable in the early 1960s: He bought a home outside the rigidly segregated "Negro" neighborhood of Wichita, Kansas.

"Fortunately, the house was near Wichita State University where the liberal professors lived so I didn't have too much trouble," he recalled.

After breaking that barrier, McAfee became one of Wichita's most effective civil rights leaders and one of the nation's most respected architects; his designs include projects for the 1996 Olympic Games in Atlanta.

While editorial page editor of the *Wichita Eagle* in the 1990s, I found McAfee a voice of conscience and a relentless advocate for social justice. McAfee's primary interest was education, which he saw as critically important to improve opportunity and equality for blacks.

As part of a school integration plan begun in 1971 under pressure from federal civil rights officials, Wichita closed its predominantly black schools and bused African American kids to schools elsewhere in town. Few white students were similarly transported.

The policy infuriated McAfee, arguing that black children still bore the brunt of white racism by being forced to enroll in schools miles from home. That meant many African American parents had difficulty attending school functions, and the kids often felt like unwanted intruders in their own classrooms.

McAfee's analysis stunned me. "Black kids learned better in the segregated schools than they do in integrated ones," he claimed. "Back then black teachers demanded that kids do their best. They told the children they had to be smarter than whites to get anywhere in life. And those teachers wouldn't tolerate bad behavior. Any trouble and the parents were called immediately."

"But white teachers let black kids slide. They don't think they can do the work," he added.

While school integration proceeded, the city pursued a major urban renewal project that wiped out a thriving black commercial district, displacing black-owned businesses and professional offices for new government buildings.

Wichita's black community was sundered. Black children were scattered in remote schools across town; the heart of African American civic and social life was turned into a glass-and-steel center-city complex for county bureaucracies.

In a conversation with the *Eagle*'s editorial board on a visit to Wichita, the Rev. Jesse Jackson said that when he was growing up in Greenville, South Carolina, his life was enclosed within an "iron triangle" of church, home, and school. Each institution supported the other, enforcing the same values and codes of conduct. Jackson noted that poor and black communities have suffered mightily as each leg of that triangle has lost influence.

For decades Americans—through the communitarian movement, for example, and books by *Bowling Alone* author Robert Putnam—have sought to recreate the community cohesion and moral support that McAfee and Jackson remembered from their youth. For a variety of reasons—dysfunctional families, loss of religious commitment, economic stress—that job has fallen primarily to the schools.

The schools can't do it all. Teachers can't be social workers, police officers, psychologists, ministers, and surrogate parents and still help kids learn something about photosynthesis or square roots. If poor children are to have any chance at the classic American Dream, the country must develop new social institutions to cope with the radically changed world of the past several decades.

For the past few decades the country has been at loggerheads over how to serve the increasingly larger numbers of low-income schoolchildren. Some people say schools should stick solely with academics. Others say that the problems of education can't be solved until the country provides poor families with a broad social safety net ensuring adequate housing, health care, and other services.

Many people have recently come to realize that both sides are right and that schools must be the focal point of a variety of functions. The umbrella term is *community schools*—places that serve as hubs of neighborhood life by offering classroom education and providing after-school programs, medical and dental care, as well as sports, cultural, and other activities.

Examples that could be prototypes for the rest of the country include the Harlem Children's Zone Project in New York City. Founded in 1997, the program provides an unbroken chain of support for poor children ranging from prenatal care to parental training to K–12 academics to college admissions counseling. A similar model, promoted by U.S. Education Secretary Arne Duncan when he headed Chicago's public schools, has placed comprehensive social services in more than one hundred schools. The plan has significantly increased school attendance and graduation rates. The Obama administration wants to expand the Chicago concept as part of its national educational agenda.

Although well-conceived social programs are crucial, research shows that the two best antidotes against poverty are a high school diploma and a stable marriage. It's almost impossible in today's economy to drop out of high school and earn enough money to support a family. The poverty rate for single-parent families is nearly six times that of two-parent families.

Another harsh truth about poverty was expressed by former Kentucky governor Paul E. Patton, a Democrat who championed school reform in his state in the 1990s: "People don't value education because they're poor; and they're poor because they don't value education."

I told my Pipkin students that I would go 49 percent of the way with them, but they had to go 51 percent of the way with their teachers to acquire the education mandatory for a prosperous future. Some colleagues said I was blaming the victim in that comment, but I felt that unless kids took ownership of their education they would not realize its importance in their lives.

Education has been called the "civil rights fight of the 21st century." But unlike the struggles of the Martin Luther King Jr. era, education today is not mainly a racial issue. Education is fundamentally a class issue, with affluent children enjoying enormous benefits denied their low-income peers.

As a teacher I had only one way to counter injustice and help my students compensate for the disadvantages they brought to school. That was to offer them the wisdom of history, to enhance their cultural literacy through stories of people who overcame the toughest imaginable challenges, to inspire them with artistic creations that spark their imagination of what is possible in their lives and to introduce them to the formative ideas that have shaped human consciousness.

I could do little about their poverty, but perhaps I could enrich their minds.

CHAPTER SEVEN

~

Faith in History

In her 2006 book, *The Mighty and Almighty: United States Foreign Policy and God*, former Secretary of State Madeleine Albright notes that her education in international affairs stressed concrete national interests. Religion did not fit in.

The dominant thinking within the American foreign policy establishment was, "The situation is complicated enough. Let's not bring God and religion into it," she said.

When Albright's book was published, the United States was embroiled in full-scale wars in Muslim Iraq and Afghanistan, as well as trying to contain possible threats from the Islamic Republic of Iran and seeking a peace settlement between Israel and its Arab neighbors.

Even so, religious concerns mattered little in crafting American policy in the Mideast and elsewhere in the world, according to Albright.

During the early stages of the Iraq war, I was editorial page editor of the *Burlington Free Press* in Vermont. Shortly after the fall of Saddam Hussein, Iraq was torn apart by horrific bloodshed between Sunni and Shiite branches of Islam. I was troubled that the vast majority of Americans I talked to—on both sides of the war debate—had little understanding of Islam or its basic tenets. I called several contacts in Washington, including members of Congress and prominent journalists, and found no one with more than faint knowledge of the bitter divisions within the Muslim world that had contributed to the deaths of thousands of Americans.

In a November 2009 article marking the end of her four-year assignment covering Iraq for the *New York Times*, Alissa Rubin recalled the violence between the Muslim factions and how poorly prepared American leaders were to respond to the carnage. A former colleague of mine at the *Wichita Eagle*, Rubin concluded, "So the lesson I take away is never to underestimate hatred or history or the complexity of alien places."

I was determined that my seventh graders at Pipkin Middle School would not be as ignorant as many top-level American policy makers were toward Islam.

To begin our unit on the Crusades, I outlined the history, core beliefs, and central practices of Islam: a brief biography of Muhammad; how the Quran was written and some of its teachings; the Five Pillars of Islam; and the religion's rapid spread from the Arabian Peninsula through the Mideast and North Africa and into southern Europe in the seventh and eighth centuries. I explained that the Sunni-Shiite split stemmed primarily from quarrels between two groups of early Muslims over which one would lead the faith following the death of Muhammad.

I added that the sectarian discord was so venomous that it inhibited Muslims from uniting against the first wave of European Crusaders trying to liberate the Holy Land from Islamic control in the late eleventh century. That same acrimony remains a powerful factor today in Muslim politics worldwide.

When the U.S. Supreme Court banned mandatory prayer in public schools in 1962, it also encouraged educators to teach religion as an academic subject. Unfortunately, afraid of controversy or worried about offending someone, most schools ignored that part of the court's decision and have avoided any serious study or discussion of religion in the classroom.

Yet consider how many of today's most significant issues are rooted in religion: Hindus vs. Muslims in South Asia; Jews vs. Muslims in the Mideast; Shiite Muslims in Iran vs. Sunni Muslims in Saudi Arabia; Christians vs. Muslims in the Sudan and other parts of Africa; Tibetan Buddhists vs. Chinese Communists, and the Beijing government's suppression of unsanctioned religious movements; the Russian government's alliance with the Orthodox Church to promote nationalism in parts of the defunct atheistic Soviet Union; the decades-old culture war between secular liberals and religious conservatives in the United States.

A sign of a sound education is the ability to perceive the world through the eyes and beliefs of another person. Studying history and religion can help develop such intellectual empathy. Lacking the capacity to transcend their own temporal outlook, people inevitably accept their society's values as absolute, the first step toward intolerance and cultural arrogance.

The Crusades were ideal to help my students develop the capacity to comprehend a civilization much different from our own by delving into the mental state of unfamiliar people who share our common human condition.

"Christian warriors, who continually and vainly seek pretexts for war, rejoice, for you have today found a true pretext," said Pope Urban II in launching the first Crusade in 1095 to drive the Muslims from Jerusalem. "If you are conquered, you will have the glory of dying in the very place as Jesus Christ, and God will never forget that he found you in the holy battalions."

How strange those words are to twenty-first-century ears: the Christian church proclaiming war, encouraging European kings and knights to welcome death in battle as an act of faith. But within the context of medieval society, a warrior culture built on raw force and fervent belief, such oratory had incredible appeal—so much so that thousands of men and women risked and lost their lives over two centuries on what ultimately proved a failed enterprise.

If I could teach my students to get inside the minds of people who thought that way, I would help give them the tools to understand much about human nature. As historian Will Durant wrote, "Theologies and philosophies, like men and states, are what they are because in their time and place they have to be."

Crusading for Stories

When I told adult friends and acquaintances that I was teaching middle school social studies, the reaction was invariably the same. "Oh, I wish I had paid more attention in history class when I was in school, but it was so boring."

Because I have loved history since early childhood, I never understood why so many people disliked the subject as kids. As a history teacher, I figured it out.

Much of the distaste for history has nothing to do with the discipline. All kids enjoy stories of the past, especially medieval tales of brave knights and wise queens, jousts and court jesters, damsels in distress and fire-breathing dragons.

A serious problem is that most middle school or high school history textbooks are flat, dull, and completely devoid of personality, not to mention lacking even the slightest element of literary grace and style.

The book I used was typical. The text covered the two-hundred-plus-years Crusades in five wide-margin pages and approximately one thousand desiccated words. Each page was lavishly illustrated: a photo of a tapestry depicting knights preparing for warfare, a colorful picture of Pope Urban II proclaiming the First Crusade, a map of the routes Crusaders took from Europe to the Mideast. The chapter's primary focus was on a few relevant vocabulary words and "key people and places"—Jerusalem, Peter the Hermit, Byzantine Empire—boldly highlighted for the fill-in-the-blank worksheets and multiple-choice tests provided by the publisher.

No real historian, I told myself, could take one of the most exciting eras of history and make it sound so trivial and humdrum. I was right. No historian did.

The standard textbooks used in American schools, I learned from a friend in the publishing business, are seldom written by the noted scholars or respected pedagogues listed in the opening pages. Instead, they are typically assembly-line products cranked out by "book developers"—companies that hire low-wage writers to hack out chunks of neutered prose suitable for state-mandated curricula. Given that the textbook is the prime academic resource in almost every subject, big publishers and a few large states that buy hundreds of thousands of books effectively control most of what young Americans learn in school.

From journalism, I know that the best way to convey information or grab people's attention is through stories. Whether found in novels or newspapers, stories are how people learn about themselves and their society. Yet most U.S. schools teach history in the most tedious manner imaginable: shallow textbooks, inane "hands-on" projects preferred by Progressive educators (an administrator suggested I have students design recruiting posters for the Crusades or perhaps, "Visit the Holy Land and kill Muslims for Jesus," I told myself sarcastically), and short-answer tests that primarily measure a student's capacity for short-term memory.

Although I had to stay shackled to the textbook to fulfill curriculum requirements, I branched out to tell students narratives from the Crusades in the hope that they might recognize how the Mideast has been one of history's constant crucibles from the dawn of time until today.

To demonstrate the enduring power of religious symbols and how deceit can inspire courage, I offered the story of the Holy Lance from the First Crusade in 1099:

A large Muslim army was reportedly ready to attack Crusaders at Antioch, an important city on the road to Jerusalem. Many of the Europeans panicked and fled aboard ships moored along the Mediterranean coast. With prospects grim, Peter Bartholomew, a French priest, claimed to have discovered the spear that pierced Jesus's side during the crucifixion. Challenged by Muslims, the Crusaders marched into battle behind the lance. Meanwhile, three knights dressed in white were seen riding out of the nearby hills; they were said to be early Christian martyrs returning to help the Crusaders. Galvanized by the lance and the apparition of the saintly trio—both events later acknowledged as "pious frauds"—the Crusaders rallied and scored a decisive victory that opened the way to Jerusalem.

History is packed with compelling and unforgettable characters, and I wanted my students to know about the two most famous leaders of the Crusades:

Saladin, a Kurdish Muslim born in Iraq, was sultan of Egypt and Syria when he recaptured Jerusalem for Islam in 1187. The loss of the holy city prompted King Richard I of England, nicknamed the Lion Heart, to launch the Third Crusade. The embodiment of European ideals of chivalry and courage, Richard confronted Saladin, who represented similar virtues among Muslims.

Although capable of barbaric cruelty—each ordered the beheading of hundreds of captives following hard-fought combat—the two men demonstrated some of the finest qualities of their civilizations. During one battle, Saladin noticed that Richard had lost his horse; the sultan sent the English king another one, not wanting such a noble adversary to fight on foot. Later, when Richard was running a high fever, Saladin sent him pears and peaches and snow to cool the fruit and speed his recovery. Saladin's behavior so impressed some Christians that they wondered how a religion they thought was devilishly wicked could produce such an admirable person.

When neither man could gain a clear triumph, they signed a treaty that gave Muslims control of Jerusalem but permitted unarmed Christian pilgrims free access to the city. At death, Saladin gave his successor advice that no Christian theologian could dispute: "Seek to win the hearts of your people, and watch over their prosperity; for it is to secure their happiness that you are appointed by God and me."

I related this story as a cautionary tale of youthful innocence and betrayal:

Stephen, a young shepherd from a small French village, claimed in 1212 that Jesus appeared to him in person and asked him to organize a crusade to rescue the Holy Land from Islamic control. Stephen journeyed throughout France recruiting followers and eventually assembled an estimated 30,000 boys and girls from all social classes, none of them more than twelve years old.

The Children's Crusade caught the popular imagination, and the youths were welcomed in high style in towns along the way to Marseilles, where Stephen expected that the Mediterranean would part for him like the Red Sea did for Moses and they would proceed on foot to Palestine. When the

Mediterranean didn't respond, two merchants, Hugh the Iron and William the Pig, offered to provide ships for the young Crusaders free of charge. Once the children left the harbor they were never seen at home again. It was later learned that Hugh and William had prearranged for the kids to be shipped to North Africa, where they were sold in Arab slave markets.

Perhaps, I told my students, such is the fate of children who don't learn history.

Legacies of a Lost Cause

The athletic teams at Springfield's Evangel University are nicknamed the Crusaders, the school's student newspaper is called *The Lance*, and its mascot is a heavily armored medieval knight mounted on a charging warhorse in full battle array.

The city's most impressive downtown structure is the Abou Ben Adhem Shrine Mosque. Constructed in 1923, with red brick walls, terracotta turrets, and twin stained-glass windows depicting a camel caravan, the Masonic center evokes medieval Cordoba or Baghdad.

I cited those two local examples to my students to illustrate the strong impact the Crusades have had on American culture. My larger point was that the Crusades were a hinge event in history that continues to have profound consequences for contemporary affairs.

The most obvious case is the 9/11 terrorist attacks by Islamic extremists. Taliban leader Mullah Omar described the subsequent American intervention in Afghanistan as "a crusade against Islam." In a 1998 manifesto, Osama bin Laden declared war against "Jews and the crusaders," linking the United States to the medieval knights in Palestine.

By outlining the multiple legacies from the Crusades, I wanted my seventh graders to understand that their lives are not isolated moments in time—that they are part of a historical matrix extending centuries into the past. Tracing the effects of the Crusades was a perfect way to teach that lesson.

The often-ignored fact is that the Europeans lost the Crusades—there were at least seven of them—after more than two centuries of warfare. But in the longer panorama of history, the Crusades put Europe on the path to the society we know today.

The Crusades laid the groundwork for modern economics, through the emergence of a banking and credit system to finance the conflict and the expansion of commerce between the Mideast and Europe. Products from as far away as China were carried by Italian merchants from Damascus, Alexandria, and other Arab cities across the Mediterranean to satisfy Europe's new craving for goods as diverse as silks, apricots, perfumes, and pearls. Wealth from trading set the economic foundation for the Italian Renaissance and created a character familiar today, the global consumer.

Travel in strange lands and contact with unfamiliar people broadened the European cultural outlook. Medieval Islam was advanced in mathematics, science, architecture, knowledge of classical philosophy, and other intellectual pursuits. Exposure to such ideas and arts helped stimulate the cultural and intellectual explosion of the Renaissance.

The dark side of the Crusades included religious fanaticism that led to the persecution of Jews and spiritual dissidents judged heretical by the church. Especially in towns in Hungary and along the Rhine River in Germany, thousands of Jews were slaughtered by zealous Christians, an early outbreak of European anti-Semitism that eventually led to the Nazi Holocaust.

Although some Muslims interpret the Crusades as an attempt by the West to colonize and dominate the Mideast, Islam emerged from the fighting as arguably the strongest power in the world. In 1453, Turkish Muslim forces captured Constantinople, closing the last chapter of the ancient Roman Empire. For more than 450 years, the Islamic Ottoman Empire ruled from the Balkans to the Indian Ocean, frequently threatening Central Europe, before collapsing after World War I.

Finally, the disruption in Mediterranean trade caused by Ottoman military success induced Europeans to seek new routes to Asian markets, ultimately prompting Christopher Columbus's voyage across the Atlantic Ocean in 1492.

From a distance of nine hundred years, harsh judgments are easily made of an exceptionally violent event motivated by religious and cultural values abhorrent to contemporary sensibilities, but I hoped the students would recognize the Crusaders as ordinary humans conditioned by their era. Poet and playwright T. S. Eliot, who often wrote on medieval themes, put it best: The crusaders were neither angels nor demons; they were "like all men in all places."

Can the modern age that has witnessed two terrible world wars and countless smaller ones truly claim to be more civilized than its medieval ancestors? Perhaps my students would eventually be able to step back, imagine themselves in the Middle Ages, and appreciate the observation of British historian John Carey, that "one of history's most useful tasks is to bring home to us how keenly, honestly and painfully past generations pursued aims that now seem to us wrong or disgraceful." No doubt the future will say the same thing about us.

I had no greater wish than that my lesson in the Crusades would give students at least a small measure of humility about themselves and skepticism toward human intentions in every era.

Choosing Your Narrative

On a September day in 1219, an unusual stranger appeared before Al-Malik Al-Kamil, the sultan of Egypt and nephew of the legendary Islamic leader Saladin. The visitor was St. Francis of Assisi, one of the most devout Christians in the Age of Faith, who was with the Crusader forces besieging the Egyptian city of Damietta.

But Francis was no warrior; he was a peacemaker. He had dared to cross the lines between the Crusader and Muslim armies on what he perceived as a mission from God. Francis wanted to convert the Egyptian sultan to Christianity.

Normally, such audacity would have cost Francis his head, but the sultan had a reputation for religious tolerance and was curious to hear the Christian friar. For a week, Francis and Al-Malik Al-Kamil engaged in intense conversation before the founder of the Franciscan order, and patron saint of animals, the environment, and Italy, returned safely to the European side.

While no one knows exactly what the two men talked about during their interfaith dialogue, Francis left the Muslim camp immensely impressed with the spiritual piety of his adversaries, especially their practice of praying five times a day. In contrast, he was appalled by the cruelty and avarice of the Crusaders.

Francis tried to persuade the leaders of the Fifth Crusade to make peace with the Muslims, but to no avail. The Crusaders were too eager for the spoils of war and military glory to listen to the saint. Shortly afterward, the Crusaders suffered a crushing military defeat and slinked home in disgrace.

I told that anecdote to my students as a counterstory to the standard Crusades accounts of massive bloodletting and hatred on both sides of the conflict. My teaching goal was to show them that people of goodwill exist in all eras and that the stories we select to interpret the world shape our outlook toward ourselves and society—on how we define our own life purpose.

A central political narrative for the younger generation of Americans will be the United States' relationship with the Islamic world. Aside from the fight against Muslim extremists, demographics ensure that Americans must deal with a resurgent Islam. By 2025 roughly 19 percent of the world will be under Islamic influence, compared with 10 percent sharing Western-oriented ideals.

To help my students comprehend this reality, I told them the original story, as found in the Hebrew Bible and reiterated in many aspects by the Islamic Quran.

It began at the dawn of civilization when Abraham sought a male heir. His wife, Sarah, was barren and encouraged him to father a son by Hagar, an Egyptian slave girl. Ishmael was born, but Sarah became pregnant and gave birth to Isaac. To ensure her son's birthright, Sarah demanded that Hagar and Ishmael be sent away; he became patriarch of several Arab tribes. Jews trace their ancestry through Isaac to Abraham; early Christians claimed to be adopted children of God on the Jewish side.

In short, many of today's crises in the Mideast and elsewhere could be read metaphorically as the continuation of an ancient feud within one of history's most famously dysfunctional families—something many of my students could relate to personally.

That story line is underscored by political commentators who see Judaism, Christianity, and Islam engaged in an irreconcilable "clash of civilizations" where land, blood, and cultural loyalties define the future course of history— a repetition of the Crusades by modern means. That narrative has justified the unspeakable acts of terrorism and torture that have marked the early twenty-first century.

An alternative narrative can be found in the Middle Ages. Although Jews and Christians were treated as second-class citizens in medieval Islamic society, they enjoyed a high level of social acceptance in Moorish Spain and some other Muslim areas. The record in Europe is less positive, although Christians and Muslims traded extensively with one another and the Catholic Church frequently protected Jews during periodic outbreaks of anti-Semitism.

The danger today is for people to take a few terrible incidents and generalize about an entire religious tradition. The three Abrahamic religions are incredibly diverse within themselves. Each faith presents a vast spectrum of ideas and perspectives that transcend any simplistic stereotype. Likewise, each faith has shown a remarkable ability to adapt to changing situations and new realities.

And while people tend to stress differences, the three faiths share some core cultural and religious values. Each believes in a divinely inspired moral code that guides temporal existence. Each acknowledges some form of life after death. Each religion honors the sanctity of the family, the fundamental obligations between parents and children. And each has reached the heights of human artistic creativity to express its understanding of transcendence.

Most significantly, unlike the ancient Greeks who thought that history was cyclical and that radical change was impossible, the Abrahamic faiths see humanity as the central character in a divine drama—that humanity can move closer to moral perfection and social justice by studying God's actions in the past.

I closed our unit on the Crusades by asking my students, "Which story will your generation pick as the best narrative for the world's future?"

CHAPTER EIGHT

~

Courting Middle Schoolers

"Mr. Awbrey, can I talk to you about something?" Mia asked in a pleading voice that meant her question would not be about the economic foundations of medieval feudalism.

"Since you are our only male teacher, some of us girls were wondering if you could tell us why the boys keep calling us hos and bitches," she said. "We're not like that, but they say it all the time. We really don't like it."

Like most early adolescent girls, Mia was wistfully romantic—in love with the idea of being in love. Every day she seemed to have a new boy's name scrawled with a colored Sharpie on her notebook; the morning social studies crush crossed out, replaced by someone who teased her in afternoon Spanish class.

But I understood her question.

Today's young people are the first generation raised in a climate of open pornography. On several occasions a boy would sidle up to me and confide that he found a particularly lewd website and was eager to fill me in. It was sad: How would Mia and her girlfriends ever construct positive relationships with these boys? When I was middle-school aged, my buddies and I might score a furtive glance at an older brother's *Playboy* magazine—in the days before photographers discovered pubic hair—but real girls were intimidating and unfathomable mysteries, fascinating creatures who prompted intense conversation over what made them tick and why we felt weird around them.

In today's MTV-saturated youth culture, such naiveté is inconceivable. At a time when young teenagers should be experiencing the first pangs of puppy love, trying to cope with strange goings-on with their bodies and disturbing new emotions toward the opposite sex, they are assaulted by sleazy media images and tawdry attitudes certain to cheapen what should be one of the most poignant—if painful—transitions in their lives.

After reassuring Mia that the boys were just trying to get her attention and that she should ignore their crude comments, I realized I should give my students an alternate vision of love and sex, one that honored women and turned semibarbaric males into sensitive knights eager to make themselves vassals to fair damsels, to risk death fighting dragons, with her smile as their only reward. They needed to hear the story of Eleanor of Aquitaine and the Courts of Love.

Love as we know it today—the idealization of the beloved, the intimate connection between romance and marriage—was largely invented in the Middle Ages. Of course, people have always had sexual relations with one another, but before the medieval era sex was used mainly to procreate or to satisfy lustful and erotic urges. Marriage was primarily a financial and property arrangement between families. What we think of as passionate romance apparently originated in Islamic Spain, where Arab poets first wrote of faithful and devoted lovers overcoming tremendous obstacles to unite in almost sacred emotional and physical bliss.

Those ideas filtered into southern France and took root among the troubadours, wandering singers and poets who entertained high and low society with tales of noble knights pursuing shy maidens. The generous patron of these minstrels was one of the most remarkable personalities of the Middle Ages, Eleanor of Aquitaine, the wife of two kings and, according to gossip of the time, a frequent adulterer.

As European society gradually became more affluent and civilized during the twelfth and thirteenth centuries, a primary task for the church and women was to contain the masculine warrior culture and control the bloodthirsty instincts of the bellicose aristocracy. The church's response was the Code of Chivalry, a set of conventions governing proper conduct and behavior for knights, such as protecting the poor, crusading for the Christian faith, and speaking the truth.

Eleanor, who inherited the duchy of Aquitaine in the lush wine region of southwest France, had a complementary solution to dilute homicidal testosterone. Along with the troubadours, she proclaimed the principle of "courtly love" between men and women as among the highest human values. To lay the ground rules for this new moral concept, Eleanor established Courts of Love.

As described by Andrew the Chaplain, a religious adviser to Eleanor's family, the Courts of Love gathered titled ladies together to define this revolution in male-female relationships and to answer questions about preferred strategies in romantic affairs. I decided to do the same with my seventh graders. Citing some of Andrew's original thirty-one "laws of love" from his book, *Treatise on Love and Its Cure*, I convened the Pipkin Middle School Court of Love.

True or False: No one can really love two people at the same time.

Answer from Kara: "False. Colton says he loves Mariah and Britney," referring to the seventh grade's top athlete and No. 1 heartthrob.

"No, he doesn't. He's just playing both of them," responded Colton's friend, Shawn, drawing knowing glances and smirks around the room.

True or False: Love invariably increases under the influence of jealousy.

Answer from Carita: "That's true. When I flirt with another guy, my boyfriend gets real mad. Then I know he still likes me."

True or False: A person who is in love eats little and sleeps little.

Answer from Marisa. "That's really true. Boys don't like fat girls, so when I'm dating someone, I try to lose weight. Then when we break up, I eat a lot more because I'm sad."

True or False: Playing hard-to-get is the best romantic strategy.

Answer from Jerzel: "Absolutely. If you chase after guys, they usually run away. You got to snub them to get them interested."

"Yeh, the guy should make the first move," Derrick replied. "Also, if she's real easy, she's just a slut. Slam, bam, thank you, ma'am." (Comment followed by uproarious laughter and affirmative head-bobbing.)

So went my most memorable class session of the school year. But when our Court of Love adjourned, I was left with the same question: Would these kids ever find true romance in their lives?

The End of Chivalry

The more I thought about it, the more incensed I was with myself. I can't let those guys get away with it. They shouldn't talk to Mia and the other girls that way. "Hos and bitches." That's pure sexual harassment, and I did nothing to stop it. The girls shouldn't have to put up with that stuff. What if it were my wife, sister, or daughter? I'd smack the jerk who said such things to them, but I let it slide, telling the girls to just take it in stride—boys will be boys, you know, that's just the way they are. Maybe, but that's not how they were going to act in my class.

It was time for some mentoring, some male bonding on what it means to be a gentleman—a strange concept to most middle-school boys, but one they should learn.

I gathered the offenders together during lunch period a few days after my conversation with Mia. I read them the riot act on how to conduct themselves, that any kind of smutty language was off limits and that sexual trash talk directed at female classmates was disrespectful and would not be tolerated.

They reacted defensively, first denying that they said anything of the sort and then claiming that the girls started it by trying to put lip gloss on one of the guys. "No excuse," I replied, "you've got to be better than that. I'm sure you were just messing with them, but don't you know how to talk to a girl?"

A few stammers . . . "um, well" . . . and embarrassed, self-conscious chuckles . . . "uh, no," responded Kelvin, signaling that I might have hit the core of the problem. Lacking inkwells to dip a girl's hair in to show their interest, these guys relied on sexual insult to send the same message.

Recognizing that my job as teacher now included counseling lovelorn adolescents, I was transported back forty years to when I presented the same dilemma to my father: "How do you talk to girls?"

"You get them to talk about themselves," he told me. "That's what every female likes to do most. Ask her about school, her brothers or sisters, her friends, her favorite books and movies, her favorite color—anything that focuses on her. Then just listen. She'll like you because you've shown you care about who she is."

In addition to my father's advice, considering we were studying the Middle Ages, I probably should have cited this lyric to the boys from my favorite Broadway musical, *Camelot*, that the way to handle a woman "is to love her, simply love her."

Somewhere between Kennedy-era *Camelot* and hip-hop's "hos and bitches," our society lost something. No group has been more harmed by it than young men. Pornography replacing romantic idealism is part of it. But it's also a fundamental shift in the male role in society. Perhaps because they are members of the first postfeminist generation and definitions of manliness are evolving, or maybe because our high-tech, brain-powered economy has less need for masculine muscle and mechanical skill, these are rough times for millions of young males.

It's called "the boy crisis"—indicators show that young American males suffer high rates of serious social trauma: mental illness, dropping out of high school, arrests, learning disabilities, placement in special education, expulsion from school. Fewer males attend and graduate from college than females.

A condition described as "failure to launch" extends these difficulties into early adulthood as many men in their twenties and thirties—the "slacker" generation—have trouble establishing themselves in careers, marrying, and starting families.

Some of the problem stems from society's rejection of the medieval Code of Chivalry: the set of moral principles and role models that for centuries exemplified masculinity. In sixteenth-century Italy, it was *sprezzatura*, the courtier, the Renaissance Man. In Victorian England, it was the Code of the Gentleman. On the nineteenth-century American frontier and in Hollywood movies, it was the Code of the West, the cowboy ethic. This man is King Arthur, Richard the Lion Heart, the Duke of Wellington, John Wayne, and Luke Skywalker; he is the knight in shining armor, the man on the white horse, the defender of a woman's honor, the uncompromising man on a mission for truth and justice, Gary Cooper in *High Noon*, the men on the doomed *Titanic* who put "women and children first" into the few lifeboats.

Mine was probably a fool's errand, wanting twenty-first-century teenage boys to practice the manly virtues of medieval courtesy. For reasons good and not, that male paradigm apparently belongs to history, unlikely to be resurrected. In its passing we have created a generation of boys totally baffled over what it means to be a man.

The Princesses Reign

Commanding the circular table in the middle of the cafeteria, asserting their authority with a ruthless combination of cattiness and gossip, the girls we teachers called "the Pipkin princesses" reigned over the seventh-grade social hierarchy.

Familiar from such teen movies as *Mean Girls* and *Heathers*, the princesses were capable of exquisite torture worthy of the most sadistic inquisitor, inflicting emotional pain that could leave lifelong scars on hapless victims. The clique's most lethal weapons: isolation, rumor, ridicule, and name calling.

Should the target of their disdain try to sit at the princesses' table, they would wrinkle their noses and wince: "What's that strange smell?" Should she flirt with the wrong boy: "I hear she did it with some basketball players." Should she wear unstylish clothes: "Did your little sister pick that out for you?" Such treatment didn't even require a plausible social crime; like a cat with a butterfly, they would tear their prey apart bit by bit just to delight in her humiliation.

For all the lectures and hand wringing by school counselors, for all the teacher workshops to prevent harassment and verbal terrorism among students, girl-on-girl bullying and hazing is epidemic in most American middle schools. Arguably, the problem has worsened with the advent of technologies that enable bullies to hound their targets into cyberspace, carrying out anonymous attacks through various social networking websites that are beyond the control of school authorities. Tragically, such incidents have contributed to the suicide deaths of several victims over the past few years.

But bullying should not obscure the dramatic, positive changes in the lives of young American women in the last two decades. In the early 1990s, a series of best-selling books argued that girls faced severe psychological damage because of the way society treated their gender. Carol Gilligan's *In a Different Voice* and Mary Pipher's *Reviving Ophelia* claimed that teenage girls suffered from low self-regard and pressure to conform to society's expectation that women be passive and compliant. Schools came under attack for catering to boys and neglecting the intellectual development of girls.

Partly because such books prompted greater attention to girls' unique needs, the situation has largely reversed. Aside from a few brainiac, nerdish boys, girls at Pipkin were invariably the best students. They controlled the school's social agenda. They had lofty ambitions, seeing their future as lawyers or teachers while the boys maintained fantasies of careers as professional athletes or rock stars. Girls presented far fewer discipline problems. They were more engaged in community life, active in church groups and volunteer organizations. Girls dominated the school's student council, honor roll, and newspaper.

Although making impressive progress toward educational equality, girls today are under extraordinary cultural coercion as regards sex and self-image. Periodically, the princesses embarked on crash diets, leaving piles of food on their lunch trays while sipping fruit juices. The slightest weight gain on a ninety-six-pound body caused high trauma: "I'm so fat!" Outbreaks of anorexia and bulimia struck every few months.

Regardless of the heated debates over abstinence-only and "comprehensive" sex education among policy makers, middle school kids are highly informed about sexual mechanics and contraceptive methods. How could they not be when Hollywood has used sex as a primary form of entertainment and the fashion industry has turned slutty celebrities into style icons? Yet, from casual chats with my students, I sensed that most teens are remarkably chaste, despite contrary impressions—hyped by sensationalist media to stimulate the prurient curiosity of adults and exploit fears of parents—that they are precociously and wantonly promiscuous.

My perception was reinforced when I chaperoned my first school dance.

"Doin' da Butt," a dance in which the girl gyrates her rear end while the guy humps behind her like a horny beagle, from the Spike Lee film *School Daze,* had caught on with Springfield kids. Several girls openly expressed their disgust to me but said they had no choice than to go along because it was the thing to do. All day prior to the after-school event, the halls were abuzz—who would "do da butt"?

I was posted at the refreshment stand to serve hot dogs and soft drinks. Fifteen minutes after the dance began, the disc jockey played the song "Da Butt" by Experience Unlimited. I watched with almost paternal foreboding, hoping one of the dance-monitoring teachers would intervene should things get nasty.

A few boys jostled each other, trying to start something down and dirty. Everyone tensed in anticipation. Nothing. I noticed Courtney, the queen bee of the Pipkin princesses. Standing with her arms crossed, she glared intently at anyone who started grinding their hips. No one moved. Despite the rhythmic bump-bump of the music, Courtney had frozen everyone in place. The DJ felt the negative vibe and quickly shifted to that all-time crowd pleaser, "YMCA" by the Village People. Courtney had kicked "da butt" out of the dance.

In class the next day, I praised the kids on how well behaved they were at the dance. Remembering that some girls felt pressure to degrade themselves and "do da butt," I also took the occasion to mention that in the medieval tradition of courtly love the woman was in complete charge. The knight writes the romantic poetry, offers gifts to the lady, eagerly risks his life for her, and begs for any token of her affection. As Andrew the Chaplain wrote: "An easy conquest sells love on the cheap; a hard one shows the cost of love runs deep."

If only Courtney and the other princesses would stop tormenting other girls and turn their cunningly devious instincts for control toward the boys.

Aspects of Love

I began my freshman year in college in the fraternity world of *Animal House* and graduated nine months after Woodstock while living in a hippie commune. Returning to the University of Kansas thirty years later to teach journalism, I was eager to understand today's students.

Although KU students still packed Allen Fieldhouse to cheer the Jayhawk basketball team and crowded into Louise's bar for postgame victory celebrations, much had changed in my absence. Nowhere was the difference more apparent than in the central obsession of most college students: the opposite sex, or—another notable transformation—the same sex.

They called it "hooking up," casual sexual encounters that when pursued on a semiregular basis were labeled "friends with benefits." Absent was what my generation called dating—a boy calling a girl early in the week and asking her to a party, dance, or other event. Instead, KU students traveled in packs, meeting in campus hangouts or downtown Lawrence clubs where things took their course.

In my undergraduate era, there was a clear linear narrative: Dating led to getting pinned which might produce an engagement and marriage, preferably immediately upon graduation for coeds seeking the coveted Mrs. degree. That romantic progression offered young couples collective wisdom in matters of the heart: parents and friends who had followed the same course could point the way from short-term passion to long-term commitment. And that's how it had been for most people in Western society since medieval troubadours turned sexual lust into spiritual transcendence and helped prompt the twelfth-century Catholic Church to sanctify marriage as a sacrament.

How quaint that sounded to my journalism students, most of whom said they had been on few formal boy-comes-to-her-house, meets-parents, and off-to-a-movie dates. For all their sexual and personal freedom, however, many of the students, I sensed, felt that something special was missing in their noncommittal couplings.

According to a 2007 survey by Michigan State University, nine out of ten college "hookups" didn't lead to serious relationships. In a 2005 study, researchers at the University of North Carolina found that teenage girls engaging in casual sex were more vulnerable to depression. "Young women are longing for romance," said Laura Session Stepp, author of *Unhooked: How Young Women Pursue Sex, Delay Love and Lose at Both*, a book title that pretty much says it all.

Although seventh graders at Pipkin Middle School were several years from the hooking-up culture, I wanted to try to immunize them against the moral and psychological hazards of such emotionally barren, cold-hearted sexual transactions. For a clue to what true love could be, I told them two of the greatest love stories of Western civilization.

The most influential scholar of his generation, called the "Plato of the West" and a founder of the University of Paris, Peter Abelard was a popular teacher at the school of Notre Dame cathedral in the early twelfth century. He agreed to tutor Heloise, the niece of the cathedral's canon. A remarkably bright and beautiful teenager, Heloise captivated Abelard and the pair quickly embarked on a torrid love affair that became the talk of Paris.

Abelard, who as a teacher in a church school was supposed to remain celibate, was so smitten by Heloise that several courtship songs he composed for her became popular among French troubadours. "Love drew our eyes to look on each other more than reading kept them on our texts," Abelard wrote in words that could come straight from a modern romance novel.

True to form, such passion must include horrific tragedy. In this case, Heloise's uncle, Fulbert, discovered the illicit relationship and tried to keep the lovers apart. Too late. Heloise became pregnant; the couple secretly married. Outraged, Fulbert, with some friends and relatives, found Abelard asleep and castrated him.

Afterwards, Abelard became a monk and Heloise a nun. Years later, they renewed their correspondence and produced one of history's most poignant collections of love letters. Sensing divine providence in their doomed romance, Heloise asked her former lover: "Your many songs put Heloise on everyone's lips, so that every street and house resounded with my name. Is it not far better now to summon me to God than it was then to satisfy our lust?"

Few people would better understand the power of Heloise's spirit-filled words than another great lover of the Middle Ages.

St. Francis of Assisi, whom we met during the Crusades in chapter 7, was born in 1182, a generation after Heloise and Abelard. Son of a wealthy north Italian fabric merchant, Francis was a high-living, spoiled young man who enjoyed chivalric poetry and dreamed of being an illustrious knight. Misadventures in war with a neighboring town left Francis in prison. Following his release, the discouraged Francis fell into a devastating depression. Returning one summer day in 1205 from an errand for his father, Francis sought shelter from the heat in an abandoned church. He chanced upon a crucifix with the image of Jesus staring straight at him. A voice told him to rebuild the church, changing his life and the course of Western Christianity.

Feeling the grace of God, Francis experienced a divine love that led him to emulate Jesus. Barefoot and wearing only a hooded peasant's tunic tied with a rope belt, he wandered around northern Italy as a beggar, ministering to the poor and sick, greeting everyone with the benediction, "May the Lord give you peace." He urged the wealthy to live Christ-like lives. He celebrated God's creation by identifying the sun, moon, earth, water, fire, and animals as his brothers and sisters.

In contrast to the bureaucratic and hierarchical church, Francis offered his followers an intensely personal religious encounter. He preached a faith of purity and love accessible to all believers, regardless of their social status, education, political power, or wealth. Salvation was the reward for sincerity of belief rather than position in society or the church. It was a compelling message that has echoed through Christian theology ever since.

Francis taught about a God not of damnation or vengeance or ritualistic practices, but one of all-consuming love—the creator devoted to his creatures.

This was my most gratifying moment as a teacher. By telling my students about Abelard, Heloise, and Francis, I introduced them to the loftiest ideals—and some of the dangers—of love.

~

CHAPTER NINE

Medieval Visions

I was told repeatedly by education professors and other pedagogical experts that today's young people tend to be "visual learners" and that television and movies are good ways to engage them in school.

The perfect opportunity to test this theory came during our study of the Hundred Years' War, the sporadic series of battles in the fourteenth and fifteenth centuries that strongly shaped the national identities of England and France.

A key event in the conflict was the Battle of Agincourt that took place in northern France on October 25, 1415. While important in its own right, the battle is especially noteworthy as the climax of William Shakespeare's historical drama, *Henry V.* I decided to show my seventh graders selections from Kenneth Branagh's film version of the play, focusing on the rousing scene when the king gives his pregame, locker-room style "St. Crispin's Day" speech to rally the English troops prior to the fighting.

Exhausted from prolonged military campaigning in France and weakened by an outbreak of dysentery, the demoralized English army faced almost certain defeat against the far larger and better armed French force. While battle lines were forming, Henry gathered his comrades and, in Shakespeare's words that have echoed through the centuries, exhorted the English to a victory that would ensure their place in history: "But we in it shall be remembered— we few, we happy few, we band of brothers."

The movie concludes with ferocious depictions of medieval warfare. The inspired English archers launch volley after volley of arrows from their lethal longbows to decimate the French ranks. The initial carnage is followed by infantry attacks using broadswords and axes to hack apart any survivors— bashed heads and eviscerated guts aplenty to thrill middle-school boys.

Afterward, I asked students to react. How did Henry appeal to English patriotism? Why did the English want future generations to recall their hero-ism? Would you feel more courageous because of Henry's speech?

A student interrupted me: "But Mr. Awbrey, we don't think about movies that way. We don't ask all those questions about them. We just watch them."

In his book, *Amusing Ourselves to Death*, Neil Postman challenges claims by many educators that moving pictures are as good as the printed word for learning. Citing studies in behavioral psychology and cognitive processing, Postman says no persuasive evidence has been found that "learning increases when information is presented in a dramatic setting." What students mostly get from visual media, Postman wrote, is that "learning is a form of entertain-ment or more precisely, that anything worth learning can take the form of entertainment and ought to."

While basically agreeing with Postman, I would not outright deny any unique educational benefit from visual media. Despite their lack of critical insight toward *Henry V*, my students learned much about medieval combat and heard a superb actor deliver powerful Shakespearean oratory from the movie. But watching a screen is easier on the brain than deciphering and digesting the written word. Flashy visuals have a much higher fun quotient than grey pages of type, but they can't compete with reading for absorbing academic content.

Much as I would prefer otherwise, my students are part of a generation that largely disdains reading. Books, aside from the occasional Harry Pot-ter or teen vampire epic, play virtually no role in their leisure lives. Their world revolves around visual entertainments—movies, television, YouTube videos, and other forms of electronic imagery—that are typically devoid of intellectual substance.

According to the annual American Freshman Survey conducted by UCLA, young people have generally abandoned recreational reading. The 2005 survey found that roughly 75 percent of respondents said they read less than two hours a week outside of school, including newspapers, magazines, books, and other publications. Likewise, data from the National Assessment of Educational Progress show that the percentage of seventeen-year-olds who "never or hardly ever" read for themselves went from 9 percent in 1984 to 19 percent in 2004. There is no reason to think that trend will reverse in the foreseeable future.

Those statistics underscore an irony of American education. Thanks to the Internet and other technologies, no previous generation has enjoyed easier and faster access to as much information as today's young people. Yet members of this generation are less competent in almost every academic subject and possess less general knowledge of the world around them than their baby-boom predecessors.

What's a teacher to do? I could forge ahead with reading assignments, assured that at least I had provided my students the chance to learn, even though most of them would slough it off or give minimal effort to complete the work. But doing so would ignore that America has crossed an educational inflection point. We are now a society in which most young people get their ideas and form their opinions based largely on what they see on television or other visual media, not on what they read in print. While books, magazines, and newspapers are still around and the Internet has lots of text-heavy websites, student learning preferences lean heavily toward imagery.

Although the ramifications of this shift are momentous—and, to my mind, potentially damaging to the nation's civic and intellectual life—they are nonetheless my students' reality. I have to educate them as they are, not as I wish they were.

In a back-to-the-future moment, I realized that this is the first primarily visual generation since the Middle Ages. In a largely illiterate era, medieval people could study subjects from philosophy to ancient mythology through images. Indeed, the greatest artistic achievement of the Middle Ages, the Gothic cathedral, could be read as a stone encyclopedia of medieval culture.

Displaying pictures of Chartres, Notre Dame de Paris, Canterbury, and other cathedrals, I walked my students through the lessons embedded in murals, portals, sculptures, paintings, friezes, tapestries, wood and stone carvings, and other "mass media" available to medieval craftsmen. Called "the poor man's Bible," cathedrals were replete with stories from the Creation to the Last Judgment, the lives of the Hebrew patriarchs and prophets, Jesus and his apostles.

Cathedral sculptors were masters at personifying abstractions. One anonymous artist portrayed philosophy as a young woman, her head in the clouds, a book in her right hand—the queen of knowledge. Paired figures contrasted moral virtues and vices: faith and idolatry, hope and despair, chastity and lust. At Notre Dame, the statue of a beautiful woman in wedding attire stood for the church, the bride of Christ.

Whimsical half-human, half-beast creatures—centaurs, minotaurs, goat men—peered intently upon the passing scene from their arched niches.

Plants, vines, and trees—nature traced in limestone—were carved into columns, pulpits, and rood screens. Animals in stained-glass windows allegorically represented elements of human psychology—the wily fox, the dumb ox, the loyal dog, the gentle lamb. Charts of the Zodiac etched into a vaulted arcade designated the divine link between heaven and earth. And, the central spectacle within the cathedral sanctuary, the theatrical Latin mass reaffirmed the sanctified mysteries of Christianity.

I passed around a small replica of a goat-horned gargoyle I bought in a souvenir shop near Notre Dame. I explained that it functioned as a rainspout connected to a gutter on the cathedral and was also intended to scare away demons. I translated some Christian iconography, the visual code that puts religious ideas into physical form: the dove stands for the Holy Spirit; the fish, the symbol of Christ; the snake, the figure of evil; the lily, the purity of the Virgin Mary.

The Gothic cathedral integrated metaphysics with stone and glass. Almost every piece of art asserted a profound lesson about faith or human nature. If American school buildings contained as much wisdom as those cathedrals, the United States would not be facing a cultural crisis.

A Medieval Art Walk

I doubted that any of my students had visited a world-class art museum. But thanks to modern technology—a computer, the Internet, and an LED projector—I could bring massive warehouses of medieval culture into my classroom in southern Missouri: selections from the Cloisters collection at New York's Metropolitan Museum of Art; Cimabue's painting, *The Madonna and Child*, from the Louvre in Paris; intricately carved twelfth-century ivory chess pieces from the British Museum, and similar riches from other institutions.

One of my teaching goals was to expose the seventh graders to the art of the medieval era, the most eclectically creative period in Western history. Rooted in wildly divergent barbarian German and classical Greek and Roman aesthetics, medieval culture was noted for making the mundane a thing of beauty. Swords, manuscripts, cabinets, and other humdrum items were transformed into dazzling art pieces.

This was not an "art for art's sake" society. Medieval people enjoyed usable, functional art, something to decorate their bodies, homes, and work places: elegant jewelry, elaborately carved wooden beds, iron lacing on garden gates. Practical people inspired by faith, they mingled the sacred and profane—a playful whale set in the margins of a hand-copied Bible; a saint's portrait on a warrior's shield; fantasy creatures woven into tapestries depicting the pleasures of Heaven and the horrors of Hell.

My primary intention for this high-tech art walk was akin to having the students step through a Lewis Carroll looking glass to a place where everything looked strange—enlarging their scope of perception to encompass how people in earlier centuries visually interpreted the world. By displaying stunning medieval designs and artifacts, I also hoped to raise my students' visual sophistication enough to reject the noxious imagery of American popular culture.

Could Giotto's series of paintings on the life of St. Francis counter hardcore pornography? Could the unicorn and maiden tapestry from Paris's Cluny Museum be more alluring than a sleazy MTV video? Could a Byzantine crucifix offer a deeper emotional experience than a Freddy Krueger slasher movie?

Despite our increasingly image-influenced society, most American schools put little or no effort into teaching visual literacy to help students make informed judgments about art and to critically analyze contemporary culture. A recent study of U.S. schools in five states by the Fordham Foundation, for example, noted that only 8 percent of instructional time was devoted to art and music, compared with an average of 14 percent in other developed countries.

According to a 2009 report by Common Core, a Washington-based school-reform organization, young Americans are falling behind their peers in other countries partly because most U.S. schools do not teach students a wide range of subjects. Focused on test taking and the mechanics of pedagogy, the report concluded, U.S. schools have "dumbed-down" their curriculum, discounting the liberal arts and sciences that are elemental to a well-rounded education. In contrast, such high-performing nations as Canada, Australia, and Japan offer a broad curriculum in history, art, literature, and other humanities.

Most young Americans never encounter Phidias, Caravaggio, or Mary Cassatt in school, nor do they hear Bach, Mahler, or Miles Davis. Instead, schools have surrendered the aesthetic education of today's young Americans to television advertisers and movie producers, pop singers and street rappers. So children become experts on the collected works of Snoop Dogg, but know nothing about Billie Holiday. They admire video game designers but draw a blank on French Impressionists. They can identify Alex Russo and every other character on Disney Channel sitcoms but are total strangers to Jo March and her sisters in *Little Women*.

I felt a special responsibility to my low-income students to stress art history and to play a wide variety of medieval music—Gregorian chants, polyphonic motets, and English madrigals—as often as possible. Most of these kids lacked the cultural advantages available to a middle-class family and were largely unacquainted with any style of music or art not promoted commercially. I was frustrated that the school district refused to implement an arts appreciation program, even though such efforts have demonstrated enormous academic benefits. Likewise, none of my social studies colleagues integrated much art history into their lesson plans, despite the fact that painting, sculpture, and other creative forms are among the best means to connect students with people from other times and unfamiliar places and to introduce young people to the scriptural, mythological, or literary narratives featured in artwork from all cultures.

Within the living memory of older Americans, fluency in art was considered a badge of the educated person, the cultivated self who was conversant with the high points of world civilization. Because most schools have discarded art history and downgraded other humanities, that is no longer the case. In effect, educators have stolen, through neglect, the cultural birthright of America's children. As a result, the historical and artistic legacy that has unified Western civilization since Greek sculptors first put chisel to marble is more endangered today than it has been since the collapse of the Roman Empire.

The Art of Enchantment

"I've seen that one" was the almost universal response from the class when I displayed the portrait of a bald-headed, bespectacled Iowa farmer holding a pitchfork and standing next to a dour, humorless-looking woman wearing a colonial-print apron and high-collar dress. The painting was "American Gothic" by Grant Wood, the most iconic image in American art.

I used the painting, named after the distinctive Carpenter Gothic window on the house in the background, to show my students the lasting influence of medieval art. From twelfth-century Chartres to Depression-era America, the Gothic style has resonated through Western culture, inspiring painters, poets, novelists, and architects captivated by the complex creative moods evoked by the Middle Ages.

Although Gothic fell out of fashion during the Renaissance, the style has undergone periodic revivals and has never disappeared from the Western artistic lexicon. The form also has taken on "culture war" overtones, attracting conservatives drawn to the religious heritage associated with the medieval period and Progressives who have used the style to express a populist reaction against arts elites. "American Gothic," for example, was part of the revolt by Wood, John Steuart Curry, Thomas Hart Benton, and other Midwestern Regionalist painters against the dominance of East Coast art circles during the 1930s.

The primary objective of my overview of medieval-derived art was to encourage my students to develop an appreciation for tradition, which can be defined as a weeding-out process that permits people to retain the best of the past while junking the rest. Seeking an antidote to the toxic dreck of youth culture, I also hoped the kids would learn to recognize the superficially trendy and give higher value to things that have withstood the test of time.

I had no illusion that much of this would happen during my students' year in seventh grade. My intentions were far above them academically, so I wasted no time pontificating about art theory. Instead, I blitzed them with pictures of buildings, paintings, sculptures, and decorative pieces that might be deposited deep within their memory banks and withdrawn when their minds had matured. "I saw that in seventh grade. I really like it" was the most I could hope for.

I concentrated on paintings by a group of nineteenth-century English artists who called themselves the Pre-Raphaelite Brotherhood and banded together in rejection of the preferred tastes of their time. Including works by Dante Gabriel Rossetti, William Holman Hunt, and Edward Burne-Jones, the paintings often featured medieval themes—lushly romantic images of knights, ladies, and heroic quests: King Arthur, Sir Galahad, Guinevere, the search for the Holy Grail.

The Pre-Raphaelites, whose name signified admiration for art conceived prior to the sixteenth-century Italian Renaissance artist Raphael, were part of the Gothic Revival in nineteenth-century England. Repulsed by the urbanization and commercialization of their era, these painters and such poets as Alfred Lord Tennyson and novelists like Sir Walter Scott saw the Middle Ages as a simpler, more reflective time when people prized spirituality, heroism, and love rather than wealth, power, and status, as in their own Victorian society.

The Gothic fervor spread quickly to the United States, where the style was favored among newly established colleges that wanted to transplant some of the aura of medieval Oxford and Cambridge onto their campuses. As seen in "American Gothic," homeowners nationwide also incorporated medieval touches—steep gables, turrets, pointed-arch windows—in their houses.

I wanted to impress on the students how deeply the medieval mind-set penetrates Western consciousness. In cultural shorthand, "medieval" has become a metaphor for religion, emotions, and tradition; in contrast, the eighteenth-century Enlightenment represents rationalism, individualism, and science. Much of American and European civilization the past three centuries can be construed as a pendulum swinging between those two poles.

That argument was framed most persuasively by American historian Henry Adams, the grandson and great-grandson of U.S. presidents. In his famous 1918 autobiography, *The Education of Henry Adams*, he wrote about visiting the hall of dynamos at the Paris Exposition of 1900. Watching the huge forty-foot-high machines generate electricity, he concluded that a new force now dominated humanity, overwhelming all that had come before.

In his chapter, "The Dynamo and the Virgin," Adams identified the dynamo with technology, progress, and masculinity; the Virgin signified nature, poetry, and femininity. The Virgin, particularly Jesus's mother, Mary, inspired the construction of medieval cathedrals and "was the highest energy ever known to man, the creator of four-fifths of his art." The dynamo, Adams said, was replacing the Virgin and as a result society was disintegrating into chaos, or worse: "Someday science may have the existence of mankind in its power, and the human race may commit suicide by blowing up the world."

But the Virgin archetype didn't vanish. In recent decades, she has reappeared in the multiple forms of the hippies and counterculture of the 1960s, the environmental movement, renewed interest in church liturgy, some facets of feminism, New Age spirituality, arts and crafts fairs, the numerous Renaissance festivals around the country, and the medieval atmospherics in *The Lord of the Rings* and Harry Potter series.

For many people, the Middle Ages offers an attractive alternative to today's technocratic society because the medieval world appears to be a mystical, charmed place. Unlike the sterile, secularized culture of postmodern America, the Middle Ages was animated by the mystery of supernatural beauty. It was a time when faith was supreme and symbols had real substance, a period when the universe moved by the hand of God, not merely the principles of gravity. It was an age that encouraged people to pursue the flights of their imagination through art of astounding creativity.

We live more by science and technology today than by art and mythology as they did in the Middle Ages. In doing so, we have sacrificed much of the enchantment in everyday life and the spirituality of nature—two aspects of existence that medieval people never lost. I would be pleased if my art lessons eventually enabled my students to view a Gothic dragon or a Pre-Raphaelite painting and imagine for themselves a world large enough for unicorns.

CHAPTER TEN

~

Miseducated Educators

Brandon usually just sat like a lump at his desk, not causing trouble but clearly disinterested in the day's lesson. Reading at a third- or fourth-grade level, he couldn't keep up with even simplistic textbook prose. His coursework was seldom finished and typically turned in without his name. Medieval Europe was an alien place he had no desire to visit.

That's why I was happy to see him tear into an assignment that asked students to build a medieval castle out of Popsicle sticks. In groups of four, the students followed a rough blueprint and fashioned baileys, keeps, drawbridges, and curtain walls out of glue, wood, and yarn. Brandon acted as construction manager for his crew, showing remarkable expertise in how things should fit together and considerable enthusiasm to spend school time working with his hands.

My first thought was disgust for the idiot who killed woodshop, metalworking, and other industrial-arts training for middle-school boys, so I was delighted that for at least a few days Brandon looked forward to social studies class. While I doubted that the assignment enhanced his appreciation of the Middle Ages, I could sincerely praise him for his effort.

Word had come down from the central administrative office that a significant proportion of our lesson plans should be devoted to "hands-on" and cooperative-learning methods that are cornerstones of the Progressive pedagogy favored in Springfield and most U.S. school systems.

I never bought into Progressivism. I was unsure what exactly the children learned from their Popsicle-stick castles—other than how to make a

Popsicle-stick castle. It was too unfocused, not pointing to a definite body of knowledge students should know.

I suspect that "project method" and other "activity-based" strategies appeal to school administrators partly because they keep kids busy and physically occupied during class time—the holy grail of "engagement"—even at the cost of academic substance. For many educators, the epitome of teaching excellence is that the classroom is exciting and fun and lessons are "relevant" to the everyday lives of children. This "child-centered" approach assumes that learning has little to do with discipline, including some sheer drudgery that any worthwhile job requires. The teacher's task is to entertain students and not force them out of their comfort zones or require them to struggle with matters that don't gel with their adolescent worldview.

My teaching philosophy was the complete opposite. I wanted to expose students to ideas, individuals, and images beyond their narrow span of experience, to expand their minds through stories and narrative visuals that challenged them to venture inside the heads of medieval people, and to disabuse them of "presentism"—the notion that today is always superior to the past.

But such methods were seen by my superiors as too "teacher focused"—I was acting like "the sage on the stage" rather than "the guide on the side." Not only that, I committed other cardinal sins against Progressivism: I "drilled and killed" to get students to learn names and places. I "chalked and talked" by outlining lessons on the board and going over them point-by-point. I "yelled and telled" by lecturing about important events in the Middle Ages.

My primary objection to Progressivism, however, has little to do with instructional methods; some Progressive tactics work well for particular students—maybe Brandon's Popsicle-stick castle will lead him to become a master craftsman. The drawback is that Progressivism has become intensely anti-intellectual at a time when an explosion of knowledge propelled by information technology demands that students be able to analyze, integrate, and make judgments about gigantic quantities of material—skills best acquired through the liberal arts.

Progressive ideas emerged in the late nineteenth and early twentieth centuries as the nation transitioned from a chiefly rural, agricultural country to an urbanized, industrial colossus. Rejecting the traditional curriculum, with its reliance on liberal arts, as elitist and too tightly focused on intellectual growth, Progressives stressed group work, social skills, and psychological development. They wanted teachers to nurture children's in-born inquisitiveness and innate desire to learn that older teaching styles were said to stifle. "Learn to do by doing" and "inquiry learning" were preferred over close reading and teacher-led instruction.

Promoted by professors at Columbia University's Teachers College, Progressivism by midcentury dominated pedagogy in education schools and most U.S. public schools. Following a brief revival of a more academically demanding, "back-to-basics" curriculum in the late 1950s, after such books as Rudolf Flesch's *Why Johnny Can't Read* and the Russian launching of the *Sputnik* spacecraft raised alarms about the quality of American education, the Progressive creed reasserted itself with a vengeance during the cultural upheavals of the late 1960s and early 1970s. This was when required texts at many education schools included John Holt's *How Children Learn,* which compared schools to prisons and virtually accused traditional teachers of child abuse; and A. S. Neill's *Summerhill,* the account of an "anything goes" English Progressive school that many U.S. educators saw as a model for the future.

As noted by education historian Diane Ravitch, Progressive initiatives "have inserted into American education a deeply ingrained suspicion of academic studies and subject matter. For the past century, our schools of education have obsessed over critical-thinking skills, projects, cooperative learning, experiential learning, and so on. But they have paid precious little attention to the disciplinary knowledge that young people need to make sense of the world."

In a recent survey sponsored by the Association of American Colleges and Universities, U.S. business executives said they want future hires to be able to communicate orally and in writing and to be innovative and creative. "Companies are demanding more of employees. They really want them to have a broad set of skills," said Debra Humphreys, a vice president of the association. Ironically, the type of education—one grounded in the liberal arts and sciences—that Progressives fought to abolish one hundred years ago is precisely what postindustrial America needs.

Since enactment of the No Child Left Behind Act in 2002, Americans have discovered that millions of U.S. children lack basic skills in reading and math. High dropout rates and low scores on the ACT and SAT college admission tests have shown that the vast majority of American eighteen-year-olds don't have the academic background to succeed in college. Yet most American schools remain committed to Progressive theories that contributed to those unacceptable results. Too many educators think that the nation's future can be built with Popsicle sticks.

Devoured by the Blob

Reaction to the appointment of Bob Corkins as Kansas education commissioner was swift and unanimous from the state educational community:

"unqualified," "right-wing nutcase," "entirely unsuitable" were among the few descriptions printable in a family newspaper.

A lawyer and political activist with a libertarian bent who favored school choice, Corkins was named the state's top school bureaucrat by conservatives on the Kansas State Board of Education who wanted an unorthodox commissioner, someone independent of the state educational establishment.

Shortly after his appointment, Corkins hired me as the state education department's communications director, reasoning that a well-known Kansas journalist could help him articulate his school agenda. I took the job primarily as a chance to broaden my practical knowledge of American public education. At the time, early 2006, I had just completed teacher training at Drury University and had accepted a seventh-grade social studies position at Pipkin Middle School that would begin in the fall. A few months in Topeka, I figured, would give me an up-close, insider's view of how educational policy is crafted on the state level.

As a government spokesman, I was a disaster. After a career of editorial and column writing, I couldn't adapt to captivity—drafting press releases and defending bureaucratic actions. Rather than hover in the background, I couldn't resist offering my opinions on educational topics to former media colleagues. Whether the issue was sex education or evolution, as long as it was controversial, I habitually shot off my mouth and angered some or most state board members.

But I came to admire Corkins. Despite unrelenting hostility from educators, he kept his sense of humor and actually accomplished a few things, notably expanding the department's data-collecting abilities and creating an office to research the most effective teaching methods. By midsummer, I had left Kansas to start teaching in Missouri, and a few months later the November elections replaced the state school board majority that had selected Corkins, prompting his resignation.

My short tenure on the state payroll taught me much about the "corporate culture" of American education. Even though I had covered education extensively as a journalist, I was genuinely surprised by what I found in the belly of the school bureaucracy. Instead of vigorous debate, intense politicking, and infighting that characterize policy making in most large institutions—colleges, the military, legislatures, law or business—education is unique in its uniform outlook on almost every significant professional issue. It's called "groupthink."

As explained by Robert J. Shiller, an economist at Yale University, groupthink is unquestioned loyalty to a specific viewpoint, the tendency to agree with the consensus. People don't deviate from conventional thought for fear of not being taken seriously and finding themselves on the fringe of their profession. The pattern is self-replicating, with senior members instilling the same mind-set in the next generation. The result is that any alternative ways of thinking are quickly squelched should they threaten the status quo.

Groupthink pervaded the Kansas State Department of Education, as it does most state school agencies around the country. Educators have built an impenetrable circle around educational concerns, creating a highly protective cartel to maintain their hegemony over school matters.

That was the crux of Corkins's problem. He was not part of the club; he had not been housetrained by the educational community. Instead, he promoted the sensible, but to many educators outrageous, concept that parents should have primary authority over their children's education, that the monolithic structure of education should be shattered to enable the growth of charter schools and other educational options that loosen the educational establishment's viselike chokehold on American schooling.

What's been labeled "The Blob," after the 1958 horror movie of the same name about a gelatinous alien organism that devours everything in its path, has its fountainhead in academia, where education professors lay down the party line and indoctrinate their undergraduate and graduate students in Progressive dogma. It penetrated throughout the Kansas education department, where I noticed that veteran administrators, education professors, and teacher-union stalwarts dominated panels that formulated rules covering professional certification, curriculum standards, assessment measures, and almost every other aspect and function of education.

Varying only in the particulars of individual states, members of The Blob inevitably share the same political objectives (don't make us accountable, but give us more money), hold the same degrees from the same (usually second-rate) universities, speak the same language of meaningless platitudes and empty jargon, and are unflinching in their determination to keep outsiders—including elected school board members—away from the inner sanctum of substantive educational power. From kindergarten through graduate school, from Florida to Alaska, The Blob speaks with one voice and pursues a singular agenda: self-perpetuation.

Since Progressivism is the only sanctioned creed, anyone suggesting other ways of schooling is dismissed as a pedagogical troglodyte seeking to bring back the bad old days of dunce caps and McGuffey readers. Never in my experiences in education school or at the Kansas State Department of Education or Pipkin Middle School did I hear a professional educator, other than an occasional maverick teacher, dissent from Progressive ideology. Like all true believers, most American educators never doubt the correctness of their common wisdom. Any deficiencies in education—low test scores, high dropout rates, functionally illiterate high school graduates—are blamed not on Progressive ideas but on the failure of teachers to implement them properly or the inability of society to solve child poverty and other social woes.

And historians call the medieval era the Age of Faith.

The Masters of Education

The two adversaries eyed each other warily. Theirs was a high-stakes medieval grudge match. Both fighters knew the opponent's strategy, having spent years arduously training in the tricks and tactics of this cutthroat game. Each understood it was the moment of truth, in several meanings of that word.

But this was not a blood-splattering fourteenth-century joust between glory-hungry knights. Instead of lances and axes, the weapons in this tournament were Socratic dialogues and biblical citations. Rather than a few gold florins from the king or a swatch of silk ribbon from an admiring duchess, the victor's prize was a license to teach.

It was called the disputation, and it served as the Rose Bowl of medieval universities. Combatants confronted one another with wit, logic, and dialectics, the winner gaining public acclaim and tuition payments from ambitious students who wanted to be mentored by the newest superstar of Scholasticism.

The disputation, which often drew large crowds, was kicked off by a senior professor who stated the question. A favorite example: Do such ideas as justice, beauty, and truth exist independently of the human mind, or are they solely the inventions of human intellect?

The black-robed warriors would be assigned a side, usually without knowing beforehand which position they would advocate or defend. They would rely—without written notes—on their study of literature, history, science, and other disciplines to support their arguments, with each man parrying and thrusting in philosophical debate that might last several hours.

The disputation was also the final hurdle for the master of arts degree, meaning that medieval "masters" (from *magister*, the Latin word for "teacher") were exceptionally well educated and possessed thinking skills of the highest order.

It's depressing to compare the medieval method of training educators to that of modern America, where few teachers pursue anything resembling the rigorous academic curriculum demanded by European universities centuries ago. Unlike aspiring medieval instructors who had to withstand withering attacks on their ideas, only a minority of teachers today possess the mental dexterity to justify their pedagogical beliefs, much less demonstrate master's level expertise in the subject they teach. Instead, they normally drift through low-voltage undergraduate "content area" courses and mindlessly absorb Progressive theory presented by uninspiring education professors whose academic background is similarly deficient.

While medieval masters could evaluate the strengths and weaknesses of multiple points of view, most of today's education professors lack insight to scrutinize their own ideological assumptions. That's why reprocessed, Coolidge-era Progressive doctrines, despite their inherent intellectual flaws, reign supreme in most education schools. Similarly, unlike the expansive freedom of thought and speech of the medieval university, U.S. education schools are renowned for closed-mindedness, shoddy research, and an almost complete lack of scholarly vigor.

For a case study in how muddleheaded education has become, consider the much ballyhooed contention among Progressive educators that schools should teach "critical thinking"—an indispensable intellectual trait at which medieval schools excelled.

In contrast to the medieval *trivium* and *quadrivium* that provided a solid grounding in language and subject matter to give students the intellectual facility to ask relevant questions and recognize defensible answers on a variety of issues, today's educators insist that critical thinking can be taught as a distinct skill applicable to almost any situation—a kind of mental Swiss Army knife. Yet, according to Daniel Willingham, a professor of cognitive psychology at the University of Virginia, "thinking is not that sort of skill. The processes of thinking are intertwined with the content of thought; that is, domain knowledge."

School reformer Diane Ravitch concurred: "We have neglected to teach them [students] that one cannot think critically without quite a lot of knowledge to think about. Thinking critically involves comparing and contrasting and synthesizing what one has learned. And a great deal of knowledge is necessary before one can begin to reflect on its meaning and look for alternative explanations."

In other words, U.S. educators reject what was obvious to the medieval mind: To think well you have to know what you are thinking about. To think cogently about history, you need to study history. To analyze science perceptively, you must learn science. To critique literature, you ought to read poems, novels, and essays.

That so many educational experts dismiss what is common sense to the average person is unsurprising because few of them are proficient in an authentic academic subject. They don't know what they are talking about because they have never thought critically themselves—they don't know what they don't know. No wonder American education is in crisis.

Until teacher-training programs are overhauled to ensure greater intellectual diversity and respect for true academic learning, U.S. schools will continue to fail American children. The dire consequences of a century of anti-intellectual Progressivism should be enough to persuade even the most blinkered education professor that things must change.

I'm not optimistic. As English writer G. K. Chesterton said, "The problem isn't educating the ignorant but rather uneducating the educated."

The Authority of Teaching

In the mid-1990s when state officials proposed raising the minimum passing score on the Praxis I exam required for a teaching license in Kansas, Ed Hammond was worried. President of Fort Hays State University, Hammond knew that a significant number of his education majors could not meet the new standard.

In an interview with me and other members of the editorial board of the *Wichita Eagle*, Hammond explained his predicament. Even after four years of college, many education students lacked the basic academic skills that the Praxis I assesses. That meant if the state imposed tougher expectations, Fort Hays couldn't produce enough certified teachers to serve the rural Western Kansas school districts that were its primary constituency.

"I can put someone in every classroom, but they won't all be certified; or I can send out only certified ones, but there won't be enough of them to fill all the classrooms," he said.

The Kansas State Board of Education chose the babysitter option, rejecting the move to increase academic demands on future teachers.

Fort Hays State has an excellent reputation in teacher education. And that's the problem. The intellectual ability of many young people majoring in education is so dismal that they can't pass a minimum-competency test. Hammond's dilemma could be replicated in every state in the country, where the vast majority of education school graduates are deficient of in-depth knowledge about much of anything—except, perhaps, Progressive gobbledygook.

Until the United States boosts the academic competence of its teachers, the country will never have a school system whose graduates are capable of competing on an international scale. Reinventing teacher training should be a top priority of today's school reformers.

"By almost any standard, many if not most, of the nation's 1,450 colleges and departments of education are doing a mediocre job of preparing teachers for the realities of the 21st century classroom," U.S. Education Secretary Arne Duncan told an audience at Columbia University in late 2009.

Ironically, the solution to the crisis in teacher education is to revive a main precept of John Dewey, the father of Progressivism. Like many complicated philosophers, Dewey has not been treated well by disciples; his ideas have been twisted into an antiacademic mélange of pedagogical mush. Education, Dewey said, should be based on "training in science, in art, in history; command of the fundamental tools of intercourse and communication." Put simply, the liberal arts. And in his classic book, *Democracy and Education*, Dewey endorsed history as essential if young people are to understand their own era: "The past is the history of the present."

Unlike his followers who have divorced subject matter from pedagogy, Dewey believed the two were inextricably intertwined, mutually reinforcing each other to construct a classroom of creativity and serious study.

In many respects, Dewey shared the medieval understanding that the liberal arts were integral to developing practical job skills and promoting civic virtues. Most graduates of medieval universities entered one of three professions: the church, government, or teaching. Those careers required people with solid educations who would accept a high degree of social responsibility, traits best acquired from history, philosophy, and other liberal arts.

The importance of the liberal arts in professional training has become apparent in such fields as health care and business. Many medical schools, for example, have used novels, memoirs, and other forms of quality literature to help improve the compassion and "bedside" manner of young physicians and make them more empathetic toward their patients.

Some business schools are turning to the liberal arts to help students adapt to the global economy. According to a January 2010 article in the *New York Times*, Roger Martin, dean of the Rotman School of Management at the University of Toronto, is revising his school's curriculum to enable students to think critically and to approach problems from diverse perspectives.

Describing his objective as a "liberal arts MBA," Martin noted that the purpose of the traditional liberal arts is to produce "holistic thinkers who think broadly and make these important moral decisions. I have the same goal."

What's good for medicine, law, business, and other professions applies even more to education. Above all, teachers should be learners. They should be enthusiastic about intellectual topics and constantly seek to expand their knowledge of the subject they teach. That's why liberal arts are imperative for educators: Those subjects not only discipline teachers' minds but also help them draft compelling lesson plans and draw meaningful conclusions from the curriculum.

Most important, educators must reassert teaching as a profession of authority. The idea that teachers should simply be guides or coaches for children is the most pernicious notion in contemporary educational theory. Most children hunger for leadership from teachers who know what they are talking about and became educators to pass knowledge to the next generation. For Progressivism to deny teachers that formative role in students' lives is to sacrifice education to childish whims and forfeit the future to the mercenary and amoral values of popular culture.

Developing well-educated and well-trained teachers and matching them with a rigorous academic curriculum concentrated in the liberal arts and sciences is the only way to ensure that U.S. schools succeed. Anything less is more of what we already have.

~

CHAPTER ELEVEN

The Hell of Denial

In addition to the disputation, candidates for the master's degree at medieval Cambridge University had to pass another special test. A beadle presented the aspiring teacher with a birch rod for smacking the palms of misbehaving students. The candidate was asked to demonstrate his competence in corporal punishment by swatting a boy in the prescribed manner. (The child received a few pennies to compensate for his pains.)

Afterward the new master received a ring to symbolize his marriage to learning and was formally inducted into the teaching guild.

Discipline has always been a major issue in education, but I couldn't help thinking that medieval masters had a much easier time of classroom management than my colleagues and I did at Pipkin Middle School.

A typical adolescent feud—neither remembered how it started—Brodie and Kelsi constantly scrapped with one another. The animosity boiled over as class was getting underway one spring day. Brodie "accidentally" tripped Kelsi while entering my room. She swung her backpack, aiming at his groin but hitting his right hip. He shoved back and hurled profanities, which she returned double-fold—both rivaling a street rapper for ingenuity in sexually laden vulgarity.

The fracas thrilled the other students, fighting and trash talking being preferred forms of entertainment at the school, providing ample fodder for gossip and a reason to distract the teacher from that day's work.

I alerted the school security officer, who escorted the pair to the assistant principal's office. Marijuana was found in Kelsi's purse, and she was sent to juvenile authorities. Brodie, however, was soon knocking at my classroom door.

"I'm sorry for what happened," a contritely acting Brodie said, unable to suppress a smirk that betrayed his insincerity. "May I please return to class?"

Under some pop-psychology theory of discipline, district administrators decided that the best way to deal with classroom miscreants was for them to take responsibility for their actions. That meant the kid would acknowledge errant behavior and apologize to the teacher. The charade was completed by the complicity of the teacher, who was supposed to grant forgiveness and receive the prodigal back into the good graces of the classroom.

The entire process was a script for dishonesty and cynicism. Students and teachers were characters in a sort of asinine Kabuki drama where everyone played their ritualistic roles without believing a word of it.

Every day it was something else at Pipkin Middle School, leading me to adopt Dorothy Parker's lament "What fresh hell is this?" as my coping mantra.

It was mid-April, time for the Super Bowl of the academic year, the Missouri Assessment Program test, the annual exam required by the federal No Child Left Behind Act. The MAP was actually nothing more than a glorified basic skills test to determine whether students could perform at grade level in math and reading. Never in the test's history had more than 40 percent of Pipkin students met benchmark proficiency standards.

The MAP does not test social studies, so I was drafted to help improve my students' literacy skills. It was back to the same technique-and-process reading strategies—classifying, identifying the main theme, circling key questions—that had been drummed into my seventh graders' heads since first grade. The kids deployed the decoding tactics perfectly. And, just like September when we ran through the same drills, many kids were mystified by what they had read. The district's refusal to implement a knowledge-based literacy program contributed to my students' difficulty with comprehension, dooming most of them to low MAP reading scores.

Due to negative consequences from repeatedly disappointing MAP scores—notably being officially tagged as a school that "needs improvement"—Pipkin teachers and administrators dreaded the test. Most of the kids couldn't have cared less. The test had no significant impact on their lives. Springfield practiced social promotion, so even the dullest student would advance to the next grade. Some of them even conspired to "goof" the test, deliberately doing poorly as an act of rebellion or revenge against the school system. Clearly, my months of sermonizing about the importance of education, education, education to their future had been just so much white noise. I thought it impossible, but many of my students were even more belligerent toward school in April than they had been the previous August. What had I wrought? Dumber and angrier teenagers?

Discouraged? Yes, but not with the students. Most of them were programmed for failure long before they entered my classroom. To educational policy makers, "at-risk" defines kids lacking sufficient economic, emotional, and social resources. To me, "at-risk" meant Jared and Tamara, Carla and Matthew, bright kids who should be on the track to college but weren't because—for reasons ranging from historic inequities in financing to habitually assigning inexperienced teachers to low-income schools—American public education has failed to live up to the nation's promise of equal opportunity for all.

These were kids whose images awakened me at 3 a.m., torturing me into bouts of insomnia and crippling self-doubt because I could not persuade them that if they tried harder they would be rewarded. But why should they believe me? Given my awareness of class and racial prejudice in America, and exposure to a dysfunctional educational system, I scarcely believed it myself.

Six months earlier, I dreamed of creating a spirited community of young learners. By April, I had developed something akin to what combat veterans call the "1,000-yard stare"—sitting immobile at my desk at the end of the day, stunned numb by what I had witnessed and endured the prior seven hours.

Other Pipkin teachers survived by gulping antidepressants or running marathons. Some built emotional filters to block the bullying and cursing, the ugliness and stupidity. Or they pursued hobbies—cooking, knitting, carpentry—to take their minds off work. A few, specifically those whose teaching was a personal ministry, never complained and calmly bore the school's toxic stress like a medieval hairshirt that toughened their religious convictions.

Neither saint nor fitness freak, I employed none of those defense mechanisms. Instead, I accepted what's known as "Horace's Compromise."

Named after a fictional high school teacher in a book of the same title by Theodore R. Sizer, "Horace's Compromise" is an unacknowledged agreement between a demoralized teacher frustrated by the inanities of American education and his disengaged students to make life easier for everyone. Teacher and students demand the least amount of work possible from one another as long as it was "good enough" to appease their consciences and satisfy bureaucratic dictates.

Sounded swell to me. I was already guilt-ridden to the gills over my teaching failures; a little more was nothing. I just wanted to finish the school year and regroup my sanity and emotional balance over the summer. I had nothing left. I was in simple survival mode.

I split the period into three roughly twenty-minute segments: Students read a section of the textbook aloud. They completed the corresponding worksheet. I presented a slideshow or video about things medieval. Tests were straight from the worksheets and textbook vocabulary lists, with a couple of open-ended essay questions for the few high-flyers.

The class kept its side of our unspoken bargain and morphed into a paragon of decorum compared to months earlier. The principal who had doubted my perseverance even complimented me on how orderly the room had become.

Although I adopted "Horace's Compromise" as an admission of my shortcomings as a teacher, the decision was surprisingly liberating. My vision of resurrecting Socratic Athens in my classroom abandoned, I no longer felt morally obligated to turn thirteen-year-olds into precocious scholars by cramming 1,200 years of history into their heads. We found a mutual comfort zone. They dutifully read and filled in their worksheets. I diligently culled my trove of medieval imagery for the best stuff, grabbing pictures with compelling historical or literary narratives behind them.

Even though it didn't conform to my pedagogical ideals, the unwelcome "compromise" prompted by disillusionment in myself and the educational system taught me a central truth many teachers arrive at—success is to never give up, make whatever progress is possible, and always show up the next day.

Esteem for Learning

My main takeaway from education school was the importance of a teacher's personal relationship with students. Kids who feel friendly toward the teacher are likely to want to do well in class. A teacher attuned to students' personalities is better able to organize lessons that resonate with them.

It made sense to me. As a reporter, I found that if I clicked with a news source I usually got a stronger, more complete story.

Normally a top-flight student, Christine had started to kiss off assignments. Chatting with her after class, I mentioned my concerns and wondered if there was anything I could do.

"How do you feel? Is everything going all right?" I asked.

She gave me a dismissive, annoyed-teenager look.

"Mr. Awbrey, you sound like my therapist and Jeffrey (a school counselor), always asking how I feel."

"This kid has a therapist?" I said to myself, perhaps more surprised than I should have been in the media age of Dr. Phil, Dr. Laura, Dr. Drew, and other celebrity psychmongers.

I backed off, not wanting to get caught up in another teenage drama queen's time-sucking, attention-seeking miniseries. A few days later, Christine was again her good-natured self, so I checked it off as another transient adolescent tempest.

Although I resisted the idea that my job included unlicensed child psychotherapy, the incident with Christine reminded me how powerful psychology has become in American education—to the point that many schools are more correctly described as mental-health clinics than academic centers.

Instead of the liberal arts that encompass the totality of human experience, most education schools today operate within the framework of educational psychology. While aspiring teachers once explored the educational philosophies of Plato, Rousseau, and Horace Mann, they are now immersed in the thinking of such psychologists as Jean Piaget, Carl Rogers, and Howard Gardner. These theorists have some useful ideas, but they pushed public schools away from instilling academic and civic values in students to focusing on children's psychological well-being.

This trend away from an academic/societal focus sprang from the revival of Progressive pedagogy in the late 1960s and 1970s. In his 1969 book, *Freedom to Learn*, Rogers updated child-centered doctrine by contending that schools should concentrate on helping students "self-actualize" themselves through a "self-initiated" process of finding their "whole person." Education should be a form of therapy aimed at "the constructive development of persons."

Under the traditional system, in Rogers's view, teachers were oppressive authoritarians who stymied a child's freedom and creativity. Children should be encouraged to get in touch with their emotions, rather than sharpen their rational side, to discover which behaviors work best for themselves and society.

Another product of the "Me Decade" of the 1970s, the psychobabbling "self-esteem" movement similarly buttressed Progressive ideology by encouraging schools to help students think well of themselves and boost their confidence—the proverbial ninth-place ribbon. For a generation, feeling warm and fuzzy about oneself, not contemplative self-scrutiny or critical examination of society, has been a primary objective of American education.

The upshot is that many of today's young adults suffer from collective narcissism stemming from their shared child-centered schooling. In their slavish devotion to popular culture and high-tech consumerism, their pumped-up egos that insist the world adjust to their needs, and their vulnerability to social-networking group judgments, many young Americans fail to exhibit the distinctive individuality promised by self-esteem gurus. The irony that "self-esteem" education produced so many unreflective, self-absorbed conformists is telling.

Political philosopher Leo Strauss described a liberal arts education as "the counter-poison to mass culture." Had educators seriously studied history or literature, they would realize that true self-esteem and individualism come from moral and intellectual achievement—putting forth maximum effort regardless of success or failure; comparing oneself to the role models of the past instead of adoring the image in the mirror; striving to act ethically to cultivate one's soul.

A primary reason for America's current economic and cultural crises—the contradictions among what we think we are, what we are, and what we must become—is that U.S. schools have diminished our civilization's core intellectual legacy. Only if it is restored can American children experience the serenity of self-respect that comes from the knowledge that they did their best.

Descending with Dante

Whenever I sought volunteers to read aloud from the textbook, Teresa's hand was the first to shoot up. She loved to read and liked the praise I always offered for her effort. A mainstreamed special education student, she didn't read fluently. Those two factors made her prime bait for bullies.

As she stumbled over words, other class members would bark out corrections. "It's It-aly, not I-tally," for example, or "You're not supposed to read the stuff under the pictures." The unwanted interference left her confused and frustrated, further complicating her task and drawing snorts, sneers, and derisive chuckles from much of the class.

Although Teresa never complained, either intimidated by her peers or oblivious that she had become the object of ridicule, what started out as good-natured teasing had escalated into mean-spirited harassment. "This is bullying," I said. "It's got to stop. Let her finish on her own." Immediately a chorus of denial swept the classroom: "No, we're just helping her." The situation deteriorated into my insisting that the aggressive interrupters were behaving like bullies and the perpetrators absolving themselves of any blame.

A hand rose cautiously. It was Nathan, a mousy, greasy-haired kid who wore the same stained, faded red hoodie every day and whose body odor smelled like two-day-old burned hamburger. He lived at a nearby welfare hotel for families who couldn't afford housing.

He stood up, barely five-feet tall. He stared directly at the class through cheap, black, horn-rimmed glasses that had been duct-taped together at the nose bridge and addressed the mob.

"Yes, you are bullying her," he said in a clear, unwavering, monotone voice, as if he had practiced and waited years to say his piece. "I have been bullied since kindergarten. I know what it means to be bullied, and you are bullying her."

He abruptly sat down, nodded at me to continue, transfixing the class into silence.

It was the most amazing act of courage I have ever witnessed. A kid who avoided the boys' restroom for fear of winding up head down in a toilet, who was constantly shoved and cursed in the hallway, taunted for his small stature and shabby clothes, had risen in defense of a fellow victim despite what I thought would be almost certain retaliation by vengeful classmates.

Nathan's heroics, however, showed that the best way to combat bullying is for victims to stand up against the attackers and shame them into seeing how their actions hurt another person. To my knowledge neither Teresa nor Nathan was ever bothered again after he defied the bullies.

I remembered that incident a few weeks later when I introduced the class to Dante's *Divine Comedy,* a defining work of medieval literature that describes the poet's journey through Hell, Purgatory, and Paradise. I concentrated on the first section, *Inferno,* because its vivid depictions of the harrowing tortures that Dante envisioned for thieves, killers, liars, traitors, corrupt politicians, and other evildoers seemed likely to stimulate adolescent imaginations. If nothing else, my students might remember Dante in their nightmares (or guilty consciences?).

Relying heavily on images from *Inferno* by nineteenth-century French illustrator Gustav Dore and twentieth-century Spanish artist Salvador Dali, I followed Dante and his guide, the Roman poet Virgil, as they descend through the gates of Hell—"All hope abandon, ye who enter here"—and proceed into the subterranean depths of the universe of the damned. Along the circular, funnel-shaped path toward the center of the earth, the two men encounter some of the most miserable creatures in Western literature. "Mercy and justice despise them," Virgil tells Dante to ward off any feelings of sympathy.

The poets see Paolo and Francesca, whose illicit love affair dooms their intertwined bodies to twist forever in a violent whirlwind. They meet robbers from Dante's native Florence, who are terrorized by venomous snakes. They find fortune-tellers with their faces fixed backwards, hypocrites wearing gilded cloaks of lead, the violent boiling in a river of blood, and gossips torn limb from limb. At the pit of Hell lies a vast well of ice where Lucifer presides, buried to his waist in a frozen circle, chewing a diabolical traitor in each of his three jaws: Judas, the betrayer of Jesus; Cassius and Brutus, the assassins of Julius Caesar.

Grabbing a teaching moment, I asked my students to create their own Inferno and list the people they would send there. Several notorious Pipkin bullies were lodged in the farthest recesses of the underworld, accompanied on various levels by "mean teachers," mom's abusive live-in boyfriend, unfaithful romantic crushes, and numerous annoying pop stars and other celebrities. Neighborhood drug addicts, alcoholics, and sexual predators also were sentenced to gruesome and hideous torments that typically involved mutilated body parts or grotesque humiliations.

For some kids, these personalized Hells proved cathartic, allowing them to impose frightful justice against wicked people, the satisfaction of pronouncing final judgment on the sinful and inflicting upon them a fitting punishment.

Although Dante would have understood this lust for vengeance, *Inferno* represents a more complex moral sensibility than merely pleasurable retribution. To Dante, the most damnable offenses aren't murder, adultery, or other misdeeds of unbridled emotion, but those committed after deliberate calculation. The criteria for evil rest more on the sinner's intentions than the results of his crime.

That's because Dante's God—like Augustine's—endowed human beings with reason and free will. People can choose how to behave and should expect to be held accountable for their decisions. Thus, carefully planned frauds, like those engineered by Enron executives or Wall Street embezzler Bernie Madoff, merit more severe punishment than impulsive crimes motivated by passion. The judicial logic is that to use divinely granted reason for wrong betrays not only other individuals, but God.

Although such ideas sound archaically medieval, they resonated with the foremost psychiatrist of twentieth-century America. In his 1973 book, *Whatever Became of Sin?*, Karl Menninger argued that modern society has suffered severely from rejecting traditional personal responsibility and guilt, substituting instead emotional distress and social factors as causes for much human unhappiness.

Echoing Dante, Menninger said, "The wrongness of the sinful act lies not merely in its nonconformity, or its departure from the accepted, appropriate way of behavior, but in an implicitly aggressive quality—a ruthlessness, a hurting, a breaking away from God and from the rest of humanity."

Founder of one of the world's most famous mental-health clinics—now part of the Baylor College of Medicine in Houston—Menninger scorned the human potential/self-esteem movement that has had such a disastrous effect on American education. Grasping the paradox that the most psychologically "liberated" generation in history is still deeply dissatisfied with life, Menninger said Americans have forgotten that "there is immorality. There is unethical behavior. There is wrongdoing."

Menninger hit another Dantesque note by insisting that the grossest sins were those directed against society, such as poverty, racism, and environmental destruction. "The germinal word that links all these sins together is hate," he said.

Medieval thinkers from Augustine to Dante are often maligned for their somber view that humanity is intrinsically prone to self-delusion and selfishness. Indeed, the notion of sin is anathema to psychologists and cultural critics who believe that most social and personal ills can be remediated through political policies, psychoactive medications, or self-help therapies.

Simply denying something doesn't make it untrue. The word *sin* may be banished from our national vocabulary, but the conditions it represents are very much alive in contemporary America. Just ask Nathan.

CHAPTER TWELVE

~

The Stalled Crusade

What went wrong?

Every day at Pipkin Middle School I witnessed the failure of American education to ensure that the next generation is prepared for a global economy and has the intellectual resources to maintain a democracy of more than three hundred million disparate and often cantankerous people. Due to some of the factors outlined in this book, a large percentage of Pipkin students will never possess the skills demanded for college or a living-wage job. They will join untold numbers of their age-group peers as human flotsam in society's backwaters, never acquiring the financial and intellectual rewards that U.S. schools provided earlier generations.

Although each underperforming Pipkin student has a unique, often tragic story that inevitably includes elements beyond any school's control, my teaching and other experiences in education help me analyze where reform went awry.

In 1989, I attended the Charlottesville Education Summit organized by President George H. W. Bush and Bill Clinton, then governor of Arkansas and chairman of the National Governors Association. In the shadow of the University of Virginia, founded by Thomas Jefferson, the nation's political leadership pledged that by 2000 the United States would be first in the world in math and science and that 90 percent of American students would graduate from high school. Those promises were incorporated into President Clinton's Goals 2000 program. Much of Clinton's plan morphed into the bipartisan No Child Left Behind Act signed by President George W. Bush in 2002 with cosponsor Sen. Ted Kennedy looking on.

According to the National Assessment of Educational Progress, the country came nowhere near Charlottesville's goal of global supremacy in science and math by 2000. On the most recent NAEP tests, 83 percent of high school seniors scored below proficiency in math and 82 percent were less than proficient in science. Likewise for the 90 percent high school graduation target. The U.S. Education Department reports that 72 percent of students left high school with a diploma in 2002, down from 77 percent in 1970. Meanwhile, as American academic abilities are declining or, at best, stagnating, foreign competitors in Europe and Asia are surpassing the United States in college graduation rates and other scholastic measurements.

The country's twenty-five-plus-year reform project has yielded some positives. State and federal governments have accepted greater responsibility for education and given schools a higher political profile. While schools once could hide their failures by combining all student scores on performance assessments, results on state proficiency tests are now broken down by socioeconomic and racial categories, plainly revealing how poorly the United States educates low-income kids. More kids attend charters, magnets, and other school choice programs. New technologies have generated mounds of data that can be used to monitor achievement and identify promising teaching strategies. E. D. Hirsch and like-minded reformers have revived the notion that subject-matter knowledge should play a central role in learning, challenging Progressive dogma that teaching is primarily technique and methodology. A scattershot of schools around the country, usually staffed by system-bucking principals and break-the-mold teachers, have produced remarkable results in some of the nation's most troubled communities.

But those limited successes beg the larger question: What went wrong?

Since the 1983 "A Nation at Risk" report launched the current reform crusade, pressure for improvement has come mainly from governors, big-city mayors, business executives, public-policy think tanks, and philanthropies. Teachers' unions, most professional educator organizations, and education schools have not been in the reform vanguard. On the contrary, the pattern after "A Nation at Risk" shows the country's educational establishment refusing to embrace fundamental change, denying obvious problems, ignoring glaring deficiencies, and rejecting almost any solution that seriously jeopardizes the status quo.

U.S. schools, in the words of historian Jacques Barzun, are enveloped in "a vortex of destructive forces." Another observer described American education as "a conspiracy of dysfunctionality motivated by good intentions."

Public education governance assures insider control. State school boards and educrats throttle innovation and thwart outside intervention through certification and other restrictive rules. Local boards of education, usually politically beholden to teachers and other district employees, serve as community cheerleaders and tax-raisers for schools while turning curriculum and similar key operational decisions over to careerist administrators. Teachers' unions use their lobbying muscle to squelch reform in state legislatures and governors' offices. Taxpayers foot the bills, and parents are marginalized as cookie bakers and sports boosters.

Because the system works exceptionally well for the educators in charge, establishment members delude themselves into thinking that schools are doing a great job and that they alone truly "care about children," in contrast to reformers who are usually branded as "enemies of public education" pushing corporate or ideological agendas. Even thoughtful, well-informed critics typically face personal attack and condescension for daring to question educators' self-acclaimed superior wisdom: "After all, we have Ed doctorates, and you don't." In effect, public schools have become a confederacy of educators who close ranks in mutual self-interest to preserve their power, confident that most critics will soon withdraw in frustration over the unrelenting resistance and take any momentum for change with them.

That scenario has repeatedly played out across the country since the "A Nation at Risk" report, leaving most schools unreformed and the public justifiably skeptical that U.S. education is capable of meeting the monumental challenges confronting the country.

Problems in education appear so intractable that the public seems to be losing interest in the subject. That certainly is the case with the media. According to a 2009 study by the Brookings Institution, national coverage of education has plummeted, constituting only 0.7 percent of news space in 2008. And the bulk of the reporting centered on such issues as school crime, budget hassles, and the H1N1 flu virus—almost none involved curriculum, teacher quality, or other classroom matters. Making things worse, dozens of school-beat reporters were laid off amid the massive recessionary retrenchment in the news industry.

Zeal for education reform also has lagged among corporate leaders who have agitated for reform. "We need to, both business and government, treat it [education] as our most important priority. It's lost a little luster and visibility with all the other issues that we seem to have on the table these days," William D. Green, chairman of Accenture, told the *Wall Street Journal* in a 2009 interview.

In his education agenda laid out in early 2010, President Barack Obama sought to reignite the education reform movement by pushing such ideas as merit pay for teachers, expanded charter schools, and a revised accountability system that focused on whether schools have sufficiently prepared young people for college or the workforce rather than on standardized test scores. But these plans represent simply another series of false starts and unkept promises unless the country comes to grips with the deep structural problems that enable educational special interests to block meaningful change.

Vice Versa on Virtues

Hands on her hips, with one hip cocked to the side, my eight-year-old daughter Grace responded to her mother's request for help at dinner. "I'm in charge here," she said in a sassy second-grader voice. "You're not the boss of me."

Later that evening, I asked my wife, "How did she get so bossy, this 'I'm too cool for the world' attitude?"

"It's those shows—*Hannah Montana*, those two twitty boys who live in a hotel, and the rest of them" she said. "For two hours she gets nothing but Disney tweener junk. They all have the same characters—absentee or idiotic parents, smart-aleck BFFs, the Casanova boy, and the doofus boy. It's always the same message—girls should want a high-glam, rock-star lifestyle with all the fashion, fame, and attention that go with it."

Mother had spoken. We banned them, every Disney or Nick sitcom aimed at kids aged eight through sixteen. Grace screeched. "I won't have anything to talk about at school. Everyone watches those shows. You're horrible. I'll do anything. . . . Puh . . . leese . . ." Her pouts, glares, and accusations of poor parenting for depriving our only daughter of her afternoon television fix lasted three days.

My only comparison is to someone shaking off a deep drug or alcohol addiction. A week, cold turkey, away from Miley Cyrus and Co. restored Grace into a child who again showed possibilities of becoming a civilized human being. She begged less about going to the mall on shopping forays. She played more with the dog. She even started reading a book. As a parental concession, she occasionally got to watch selected episodes from her mother's collection of *The Gilmore Girls*.

According to *Psychology Today*, roughly three-fourths of American parents believe that the materialism and negative influences from television, movies, and music present serious problems in rearing children. More than 85 percent of the parents surveyed believe that sexual content in the media contributes to children becoming sexually active, and violence increases aggressive behavior in kids.

Before having children, I would have berated parents for their failure to monitor their kids' viewing and listening habits. As a father, I know it is not that easy. I'd rather face the fangs of Dante's dogs of Hell than suffer again through Grace's prolonged howl-fest over losing *The Witches of Waverly Place*.

I've delivered my jeremiad against popular culture elsewhere in this book, but the values and lessons the mass media convey to our children sabotage almost any chance that the United States can create the public education system that ensures the economic and academic well-being of today's children. Entertainment moguls and marketers show no shame or decency in promoting attitudes directly contrary to the best interests of society and children. When kids bring the sleazy, commercialized, anti-intellectual, and narcissistic values of the entertainment industry to school, teachers are virtually powerless to inspire a more lofty vision of life. It's Gresham's Law applied to morality—the polluted drives out the pure.

Like their colleagues in other parts of the country, Springfield business leaders have taken note, largely because they have become appalled by the slovenly work habits, poor academic skills, and entitlement attitudes of many of their prospective employees.

Meet Character Ed, a pixielike cartoon personality who represents a communitywide character education initiative sponsored by the Springfield Area Chamber of Commerce and the Springfield Public Schools. Yes, the ethical formation of the children of Springfield—and the district's only comprehensive effort in moral reasoning—is a project of local business leaders who worry that schools are not producing disciplined, competent, and reliable workers.

Launched in 2005, Character Ed spotlights one behavioral trait per month such as Respect, Courtesy, Cooperation, Dependability, Responsibility, and Caring.

It worked this way. A graduate student in counseling at Missouri State University would take over my class for a half hour to instill that month's virtue in the kids; for example, Honesty. He asked the kids about lies, the difference between white and more serious lies, and why they should always tell the truth to parents, teachers, and others in authority. The telltale yawn, the turned-down eyes, the giggles at nothing: The kids weren't buying it. Their moral universe was pragmatic. Get away with whatever you can. The scam: that's what it's about on almost every television news or entertainment program.

One month, realizing that this was going nowhere, I put another list on the board after the trainer left, the Seven Virtues the early Middle Ages compiled from classical and Christian sources: Prudence, Justice, Restraint, Courage, Faith, Hope, and Love. Even seventh graders recognized the greater moral heft of the medieval virtues as compared with Character Ed's list.

Until the Progressive era of the early twentieth century, moral instruction within the same cultural lineage as the Seven Virtues was the centerpiece of American education. The goal was to shape character, foster civic involvement, preserve the community's heritage, uphold teachers as models of intellectual and moral integrity, and encourage personal responsibility and autonomy. Such words as *soul, wisdom, truth*, and *learning* were etched in stone over school portals, in total sincerity without taint of sitcom irony or cynicism. It used to be called common morality; now, sociologists label it with a hoary pejorative, the Puritan ethic.

The failure of U.S. society to produce morally and intellectually capable citizens could prove calamitous. In his 2009 book, *Intelligence and How to Get It*, Richard Nisbett, a psychology professor at the University of Michigan, argues that cultural distinctions largely determine the fate of a society or ethnic group. Citing Asian Americans, West Indian blacks, and Jews as three highly successful examples, Nisbett found that each puts a high premium on education and family cohesion. Jews, for instance, have a deep reverence for learning that originated from reading scripture fervently; Chinese and other Asians benefit from the Confucian stress on family, scholarship, and personal propriety.

Questions: Hannah Montana or Confucius? Who is the best moral guide for a nation's children? Which one is idolized by millions of young Americans?

Nisbett also says that intelligence is largely acquired and not as dependent on genetics as once believed. Schools and education matter. Children exposed to academically solid instruction and who develop good work habits and mental qualities have the greatest chance of becoming well-educated and productive citizens.

America once had an abundance of public schools strikingly similar to the kind Nisbett envisions: rigorous curricula, authoritative teachers, and nurturing communities that made U.S. public education a global model for scholastic achievement and civic commitment. Regenerating that time-proven intellectual and moral legacy might be the most important task for reformers charting America's educational future.

Common Classroom Culture

In the spring of 1895 some students in Saline County, Kansas, most of them children of cowboys, dirt farmers, Swedish immigrants, or small-town tradesmen, took their final exam to pass eighth grade. The test included the following questions:

Grammar:

- Name the parts of speech and define those that have no modifications.
- What are the principal parts of a verb? Give principal parts of *do*, *lie*, and *run*.
- Define verse, stanza, and paragraph.

Arithmetic:

- Find the cost of 6,720 lbs. of coal at $6.00 per ton.
- District No. 33 has a valuation of $35,000. What is the necessary levy to carry on a school seven months at $50 per month, and have $104 left over for incidentals?
- Find the interest on $512.60 for 8 months and 18 days at 7 percent.

U.S. History:

- Show the territorial growth of the United States.
- Relate the causes and results of the Revolutionary War.
- Who were the following: Morse, Whitney, Fulton, Bell, Lincoln, Penn, and Howe.

Geography:

- How do you account for the extremes of climate in Kansas?
- Name all the republics of Europe and give capital of each.
- Describe the movements of the earth. Give inclination of earth.

Only a few Pipkin Middle School students, and not that many more of today's average high school graduates, could pass an updated test with a comparable degree of difficulty to the one given to those nineteenth-century Kansas eighth graders.

The Saline County exam is depressing evidence of what Progressive dogma has done to American education, taking what in 1895 was—aside from the unconscionable racism of the era—the world's best public school system and reducing it to a global embarrassment that has relegated millions of children close to the intellectual and cultural level of medieval serfs.

Ironically, the Saline County questions expected nineteenth-century students to have exactly the academic skills—critical thinking, problem solving—that contemporary educators insist are needed but are severely lacking in today's young Americans. The full range of Benjamin Bloom's Taxonomy—from knowledge to evaluation—is covered in a test written decades before the University of Chicago professor developed his hierarchy of thinking that is a template of modern education.

At the time the eighth-grade exam was given in Saline County, my great-grandmother, Nellie Martin, was teaching elementary school sixty miles south in Hutchinson, Kansas. Her story is typical of thousands of school-marms of the era.

After graduating from high school in Illinois at age seventeen, Nellie was told by her brother, a lawyer in Hutchinson, that they needed teachers in that growing prairie town. She traveled west, got a job at Sherman School, met a young former math teacher also from Illinois who was "reading law" in her brother's office, married him, and continued teaching for many years.

As a child in Hutchinson, I heard stories from bankers, attorneys, business leaders, and other community members about Nellie. Partly by stressing proper use of "the queen's English," she turned frontier kids from grungy ragamuffins into civically literate citizens able to govern a boisterous cattle-raising, wheat-farming, salt-mining, railroading Western Kansas town.

Nellie Martin would not be welcome in a modern American school. She lacked official credentials. All she had was a solid high school education, a love of kids, and a passion for teaching. Yet her students went on to help win two world wars, survive a ruinous economic depression, and raise the United States to undisputed global economic and political supremacy.

The nation's public education system was established for two overriding purposes: to make Americans out of the most divergent collection of people ever assembled within the borders of one country and to ensure that they would live under a resilient republican form of government. To that end, leaders such as Thomas Jefferson and Abraham Lincoln advocated and teachers like Nellie Martin taught a core curriculum that inculcated democratic ideals and virtues.

Due primarily to the Progressive deemphasis of history, literature, and other liberal arts, the country no longer has a coherent curriculum that helps unify the nation socially and politically and prepares young people for civic life. No longer does the educational system focus on creating, in the words of Jacques Barzun, "a community of minds, a culture—indeed, a society in the original sense of the word, which is: a group of companions."

The United States has a—perhaps last—chance to ensure that, despite differences in class, race, and ethnicity, young Americans acquire a basic set of values that transcend diversity and help articulate a shared national purpose. Under the leadership of the National Governors Association and the Council of Chief State School Officers, educational experts released in 2010 consensus blueprints of what American students should know in math and English, including such basic documents as the Declaration of Independence and Lincoln's Second Inaugural Address. The intention is for states to take those standards and use them as a general blueprint for their school systems, ensuring decentralized control of education and easing fears that the federal government would create a national curriculum that could be manipulated by one or another political or ideological faction.

More than two hundred years ago, Thomas Jefferson encouraged a common curriculum so children's "memories may here be stored with the most useful facts from Grecian, Roman, European and American history." Jefferson and other traditionally educated founders understood that the liberal arts were the intellectual core of American greatness; without their retrieval it's doubtful the country will retain that heritage.

CHAPTER THIRTEEN

~

People of History

If you want to spark a seventh grader's interest in a classic of English literature, start with a fart joke.

As the story goes, a friar asks a man for some money. The man agrees and says he keeps some coins under his rear end. He tells the friar to reach down and take what he wants. When the friar does so, the man rips a boomer. "No cart horse could produce a fart of such a sound," the narrator says.

That gag is one of dozens in Geoffrey Chaucer's *Canterbury Tales*, the fourteenth-century account of twenty-nine pilgrims traveling from London to the holy shrine of "the blissful martyr" St. Thomas Becket, who was murdered by four knights in Canterbury Cathedral in 1070 for defying King Henry II. In the intervening centuries, the site had become popular with medieval spiritual tourists offering penance for their sins or simply searching for adventure away from home.

I picked *The Canterbury Tales* as the ideal lesson to close out the class's study of the Middle Ages. To read Chaucer is to be carried back into history, to see the clothing, smell the food, and hear the cadences of a language that has evolved into our own. Although products of Chaucer's imagination, the pilgrims come across as no different from ourselves—sometimes profane, coarse, and unmercifully cruel but equally often devout, generous, and immensely likable.

Chaucer's stories and characters were perfect to help my students identify with people who lived more than six hundred years ago and to realize that human nature has changed not a whit over the centuries. Humor, that uniquely human trait, is especially good at transcending time and place. Indeed, in what era have teenaged boys not enjoyed a silly fart joke?

Chaucer starts his poem at a tavern outside London where the pilgrims, who represent a cross section of late fourteenth-century English society, have gathered to begin their medieval package vacation. To relieve the tedium of the journey, the host proposes that each person tell a story. The traveler with the best tale would win a free dinner at the end of the trip.

Selecting carefully to avoid some of the most bawdy stories in the English language, I told my students a few of the tales, such as this one from the Wife of Bath, the five-times married protofeminist whose larger-than-life personality has for centuries inspired countless novels, plays, films, and doctoral dissertations:

> A knight from King Arthur's court sexually assaults a woman, a crime punishable by death. Queen Guinevere intervenes, and the king turns the case over to her for judgment.
>
> The queen sends the knight on a quest to discover what women want "more than anything else." If his answer displeases the queen, he will be executed. For a year, he interviews numerous women but never receives the same response. He finally encounters an old hag who says she will give him the correct answer, but for payment he must grant her an unspecified request.
>
> The knight agrees and returns to court with the woman, where the queen pardons him after he explains that what women want is control over their husbands. As her reward, the old woman demands that the knight marry her. On their wedding night, the man admits unhappiness because his new wife is ugly. She reacts by offering him a choice: she will be unattractive but faithful to him or beautiful but disloyal. He asks her to make the decision. Pleased with such power, the hag becomes faithful and fair and the couple lives happily ever after.

Written between 1387 and 1400, *The Canterbury Tales* has special immediacy for a six-century-old book because it is the first major piece of English literature intelligible to our contemporary ear. From Chaucer and his band of pilgrims descend the glories of Shakespeare, Milton, and hundreds of other writers who have helped make English the universal language of our day—the Latin of the twenty-first century.

But modern English is only one of the lasting legacies from the Middle Ages. Some of contemporary society's most noteworthy debts to that one-thousand-year era that took Western Europe from post-Roman Empire barbarism and ignorance to the cultural and intellectual explosion of the Renaissance include the following:

- *The modern legal system.* The medieval period developed civil law, maritime and commercial codes, the jury system, and the concept of habeas corpus. When English aristocrats forced King John to sign the Magna Carta in 1215 they unwittingly laid the foundations for American democracy and representative government.
- *The capitalist economic system.* Medieval people organized an international banking and trading structure and created craft guilds that became models for modern labor unions. The constant search for new markets, new lands, or new excitements led medieval Europeans to explore the world—from Marco Polo in China to Leif Ericson in North America.
- *The academic legacy.* At typical U.S. college graduations, professors confer degrees—bachelor's, master's, doctoral—that originated in medieval universities and dress in robes and other regalia reminiscent of the Middle Ages. Minds disciplined by Scholastic philosophy shaped the skeptical, inquiring Western intellectual tradition that is known for applying penetrating logic and reason to every question.
- *Modern science.* The experimental methods and observations of Robert Grosseteste, bishop of London, and Franciscan friar Roger Bacon in the thirteenth century set the course for modern science. Europe's adoption and refinement of Arabic and Indian mathematics led to development of the decimal system and breakthroughs in geography, astronomy, and optics. Such inventions as the pendulum clock and the compass radically altered conceptions of time and space. The saddle stirrup and other European military technologies gave medieval armored knights an insurmountable edge in warfare that Western nations have held ever since.
- *Arts and architecture.* Majestic Gothic cathedrals united theology, architecture, painting, and poetry to express a form of human creativity that still resonates from the awesome height of an urban skyscraper to the glowing warmth of the stained-glass windows in a country church. Medieval tapestries, embroidery, and other crafts reflect distinctly artistic touches that remain popular today.
- *Languages and letters.* In literature, the Middle Ages gave birth to Italian, French, English, and other European vernacular languages. Dante and Chaucer rival the finest poets of any literary era. No historical period or culture has produced writings more enchanting than the Arthurian legends. And it's impossible to envision modern romance novels and movies without the erotically charged love songs of French troubadours.

For most of my students, seventh-grade social studies would be the last time they encountered the Middle Ages in a classroom. Sadly, there was much I failed to give them, partly because of my inadequacies as a teacher and partly because of their aversion to anything that smacked of schoolwork. But I hoped they would at least remember a bit about Charlemagne, Eleanor, Francis, and Chaucer's fictional wayfarers. Because it is not facts or dates that make history, but people like us—real or imaginary.

Paths to the Grave

Several years ago, I visited Belgrade, the capital of Serbia, and toured the Kalemegdan Citadel. Strategically perched on a bluff overlooking a bend in the Danube River, the citadel had been a military fortress since the third century BC, when Celts controlled the area. Over the centuries the site has been occupied by successive waves of Romans, Huns (rumor has it that the great warrior Attila, "the scourge of God," is secretly buried on the grounds), Goths, Byzantines, Ottomans, Bulgarians, Austrians, Hungarians, and, during World War II, Germans.

Wandering about the citadel, I noticed a small stone structure with what to me was unintelligible script carved above the doorway. Curious, I peeked inside and found only a few dirt-encrusted rakes, hoes, and other tools propped against the side walls. I then saw a sign saying the building was originally the tomb of a Turkish sultan, a mighty potentate when the Islamic Ottomans ruled the Balkans.

Now, it was simply a dilapidated gardener's shed.

I immediately thought of my favorite poem, John Gray's "Elegy Written in a Country Churchyard," which includes a memory verse that has been part of my personal philosophy since I first read it in high school.

> The boast of heraldry, the pomp of power,
> And all that beauty, all that wealth e'er gave,
> Awaits alike th' inevitable hour:
> The paths of glory lead but to the grave.

Spending most of my career in the ego-driven worlds of media and politics, I have frequently recalled Gray's "Elegy" as a corrective. It reminds me that life is transitory, that earthly vanities and ambitions—the now-ignored portrait of a forgotten politician inside the courthouse; the prize-winning newspaper reporter's clips moldering in a library archive—are ultimately meaningless.

It is the same point underscored by another of my life-directing poems, "Ozymandias" by Percy Bysshe Shelley. Encountering a broken statue, "a colossal wreck," scattered across a desert wasteland, its shattered head lying half sunk in the sand, a traveler reads this inscription on the pedestal:

"My name is Ozymandias, king of kings:
Look on my works, ye Mighty, and despair!"

As reported by the Venerable Bede, a monk who is considered the father of English history, during a meeting in the early seventh century between Christian missionaries and the pagan King Edwin of Northumbria, a royal advisor used this metaphor to describe human life:

Think of the sparrow flying through a warm, brightly lit room during a winter evening. While the bird is inside, he is safe from the harsh weather, but once he leaves, he vanishes into the dark of the cold night. "So this life of man appears for a short space, but of what went before or what is to follow we are ignorant," the aide concludes.

Gray, Shelley, and the unnamed Anglo-Saxon noble seem to agree that while we may have moments of pleasure or power, our personal destiny is death and, for most of us, historical oblivion.

Is there any larger meaning to history that gives our lives an overriding purpose beyond merely surviving our biblical three score and ten years? That question has perplexed humanity since our species became aware of time. Can we discern something from past civilizations to give us clues to the fate of our own?

According to ancient Greeks and Romans, history was cyclical, doomed to repeat itself with fatalistic regularity. "There will also be other wars, and the great Achilles will again be sent to Troy," wrote the Roman poet and Dante's underworld guide, Virgil.

In contrast, Augustine argued that history is predetermined, the gradual unfolding of God's master plan for humanity. Divine intent infuses every event, however obscure or ambiguous it may seem to human intellect. In the fullness of time, all will be revealed and understood.

In the nineteenth century, such philosophers as G. W. F. Hegel, Karl Marx, and Comte de Saint-Simon detected various natural patterns and laws that to them suggested an underlying dialectical logic to the course of history.

After the cataclysm of World War I, German historian Oswald Spengler said civilizations traced a predictable life course that traveled through several stages of cultural cohesion to eventual and unavoidable disintegration.

I have been intrigued by questions surrounding human fate since I was thirteen years old and heard a lecture by British historian Arnold Toynbee. At the time, the early 1960s, Toynbee was a visiting professor at Grinnell

College in Iowa, where my eldest sister was a student. Attending an appearance by Toynbee, I was mesmerized by the breadth of his knowledge, even though I could scarcely follow his broad sweep through the history of civilizations since the Sumerians planted the first cities in Mesopotamia. When I was old enough, I read an abridged version of his masterpiece, the twelve-volume *A Study of History*. From then on, I have perceived the world through largely Toynbee's eyes.

Toynbee interpreted history in terms of challenge and response. Civilizations rose to meet specific difficulties, which could range from natural disasters to threats from foreign invaders to an economic or political crisis. A civilization's survival hinged on whether it could continue to overcome successive dangers; if not, it would perish. For me, Toynbee's most convincing example was when the Catholic Church converted the barbarian tribes to Christianity following the collapse of the Roman Empire, thus ensuring the cultural unity of Western Europe.

Toynbee's most famous quotation is that "Civilizations die from suicide, not by murder." The survival of Western civilization depends on us, the living, passing our society's traditions and ideals to our children. In that cultural transmission lays our primary hope for immortality. This brings up the worrisome situation facing the United States in the twenty-first century.

Over the past century, the United States has courageously confronted at least three existential threats: the Great Depression of the 1930s, Nazi despotism in World War II, and the communist challenge from the Soviet Union during the forty-plus-year Cold War. Today, the country's two most pressing dangers are less overt or dramatic but equally daunting: the global economic rivalry with China and other emerging nations and the failure of U.S. society—especially our public school system—to provide the moral virtues, civic values, and practical knowledge necessary to maintain American democracy and economic prosperity.

My fear is that when I looked inside the Turkish sultan's tomb in Belgrade, I saw the fate of America—a monument to power and grandeur desecrated and forgotten when the course of human civilization moved elsewhere.

Sic transit gloria mundi—"Thus passes the glory of the world."

The Renaissance Arrives

Without any introductory comment to the class, I displayed a picture of Michelangelo's statue of David, a monumental work that depicts the future king of ancient Israel in full frontal nudity moments before his biblical battle with Goliath.

Snickers rippled around the room as the students noticed David's cir-
cumcised genitals, heavily muscled arms, washboard abs, and self-assured
confidence about his task ahead.

"As you can see, we are no longer in the Middle Ages," I said in a deadpan
voice, referring to the stone-and-stained-glass parade of Virgin Marys, baby
Jesuses, and heavily robed and bearded religious figures I showed the class
during our lessons in medieval art. "We are now in the Renaissance," I added
matter-of-factly. "Do you see how attractive—even sexy—the male body can
be? That's something you didn't have in the Middle Ages."

"He's hot," Courtney nodded approvingly, drawing nervous laughter,
mostly from boys uncomfortable with the notion of an erotically alluring
naked male.

I waited a second—for someone to shout, "It's so gay."

Silence. Complete quiet. I ventured deeper. "Though I'm straight, this
statue of David reminds me that I have been captivated by the beauty of
another man."

I told about covering Muhammad Ali's boxing match against Jimmy
Young in April 1976 at the Capital Center outside Washington, D.C., when
I was a UPI sports reporter early in my journalism career. I spent several days
hanging around Ali's training camp doing prefight stories and saw the champ
beat Young in a fifteen-round decision. Although Ali, at 230 pounds, was at
the heaviest weight of his career and not in the best condition (he loved ice
cream), he still was jaw-dropping gorgeous—the flesh-and-blood virility of a
Michelangelo marble.

"So, yeh, I can see how a man can fall in lust with another guy," I said,
noting that male homosexuality was widely practiced in Florence, Venice,
and other Italian cities during the Renaissance, despite periodic persecution
by authorities.

That said, I dropped the subject, though I hoped my comments would
moderate some of the homophobia rampant at Pipkin Middle School.

My man-crush on Muhammad Ali gave me an inkling of how some Europeans might have reacted to the intellectual and cultural awakening that
exploded in fifteenth-century Italy. Although people at the time never knew
the term *Renaissance*, which was first used by French historian Jules Michelet
in 1858 to separate the Middle Ages from the modern age, they understood
they were living through a transformative era that brought new ways of looking at everything from political philosophy to the masculine physique.

Between the barbarian chaos that followed the collapse of the Roman
Empire and the massive destruction and wholesale human slaughter of the
twentieth century, the fourteenth century was the most terrible period in

Western history. The Black Death, a continentwide plague linked to flea-infested rats that arrived in Italy in 1347 on a boat from the Middle East, eventually killed up to one-third of the population of Western Europe. The Hundred Years' War between England and France raged intermittingly most of the century, wiping out much of the aristocratic warrior class and devastating once-productive farmland and bustling villages. A major shift in the weather, characterized by harsh winters and rainy and cold summers, induced decades of widespread famine. These factors dropped the life expectancy of the average English citizen from roughly thirty-five years in 1278 to around seventeen years in 1375.

But a new Europe emerged from those horrors. The feudal system was demolished. The mounted, armored knight as the basis of military power was replaced by the English longbow and the refinement of gunpowder to knock down castle walls. Labor shortages from the great plagues and demands for reform during several bloody peasant revolts led to increased wealth and personal liberty for millions of former serfs.

Although these changes upended the medieval social and economic structure, they can't alone account for the upheaval that turned the worn-out Age of Faith into one of the most innovative, energetic, and intellectually sparkling eras of human history.

While historians argue when the Renaissance began, a date as good as any is the winter of 1397 when Byzantine scholar Manuel Chrysolaras arrived at the University of Florence to teach the Greek language. For the first time in more than seven hundred years Greek was studied in Italy. Soon texts unknown in Western Europe by Plato, Aristotle, and other ancient Greek philosophers, playwrights, and writers found their way onto newly invented printing presses and into the hands of eager readers in Italy and elsewhere. The fall of the Byzantine Empire with the Muslim conquest of Constantinople in 1453 prompted hundreds of Greek scholars to flee westward, bringing additional knowledge with them.

As with the revival of formal education by Alcuin and Charlemagne in the eighth century, this cultural rebirth was led by scholars dedicated to the liberal arts. For example, in his 1451 book, *The Education of Children*, Pope Pius II advocated teaching history, geography, and classical literature to promote "enlightened intelligence." Equipped with such knowledge, Renaissance Europeans produced some of humanity's most lasting and compelling artistic, literary, scientific, and philosophical achievements, leaving a creative legacy unrivalled before or since.

Sadly, such an education is in disfavor among people who control American schooling. Rather than encourage children to study the past—to explore the human record of triumphs and mistakes—today's Progressive ideologues define education mainly through a mantra of fuzzy, incoherent buzzwords lacking intellectual integrity: "learning to learn," "critical thinking," "problem solving," and so forth. They have adopted a social-science mind-set that classifies teaching as a formal skill, the proper application of specific instructional methodologies, instead of a profoundly humanistic enterprise in which an adult extends cultural and academic enlightenment to children.

Cultural critic Camille Paglia put it best: A teacher should become "a bard, a living archive and singer of sagas." That is, teachers should be narrators of the human drama, storytellers helping young people recognize that they are part of the marvelous historical adventure called human civilization.

Tragically, such awareness is increasingly rare among young Americans, as are teachers who are intellectually able to communicate humanity's cultural heritage to the next generation. Unless the U.S. education system resuscitates the humanistic tradition that carried Western civilization from Plato's Academy in ancient Greece to the one-room schoolhouse of nineteenth-century America, today's children will succumb to a fearful barbarism, a fragmented, disempowered, and isolated generation lacking moral, spiritual, or historical purpose.

CHAPTER FOURTEEN

~

What the Teacher Learned

The phone rang at dinnertime on Christmas Eve of the next year. I expected another pesky telemarketer.

"Hi, Mr. Awbrey," said the menacingly familiar voice. "This is Marshall Perry. Remember me from Pipkin?"

Caught totally off guard, I thought to myself: Remember? How could I forget the kid who almost drove me out of teaching before the end of my first month on the job?

"Why, Marshall, of course I remember you," I replied gamely. "I'm just really surprised to hear from you. How are you doing?"

"Oh, about the same," he replied in the wiseacre tone that still echoes in my mind when I think about Pipkin. "I've been kicked out of Central High School for the same stuff I pulled in your class."

"So you never did get it together and try to make something of yourself," I responded in a matter-of-fact, tough-love way. "Sad to hear it. You really have potential. You're bright, quick, clever. But you know that. Everyone tells you that."

"Yeh, yeh, I know. I know. I know." he said.

"I'm calling because I wanted to say I'm sorry for all the problems I caused you. At first I thought you were just another crappy teacher, hassling me about anarchy and calling me out all the time, but then I realized you really were trying to help me."

What's going on, I wondered, is he in some bad-boy twelve-step program that requires apologies to people he pissed off? "Marshall, is this for real? That was more than a year ago."

"I don't know. I was just thinking about you and decided I had to say that," he responded.

We chatted a bit longer. Things hadn't changed much. Despite hours of professional counseling, megadoses of mood and mind-altering medications, and the tears and pleas of his cancer-survivor mother, Marshall was still brash and defiant. Unable to stomach the routines of high school any better than middle school, he was aiming for a place in Springfield's lone alternative school, which already had a lengthy waiting list of dropouts and misfits who don't conform to the standard school program.

I told him I had left teaching to write a book about education based partly on my Pipkin experience. "You will certainly be in it," I added.

"Way cool. Make me famous, will you?" he replied, followed by an awkward silence . . .

"Well," he broke in, "I just wanted to say that I appreciate what you tried to do for me."

"That means a lot to me," I said.

And it did. I might not have transformed a troubled kid, but I had shown that I truly cared about him. A small victory, perhaps, but one I will always cherish.

When I was a reporter, it was easy to walk away once the story made the next morning's newspaper—after the accident victim went to the hospital, the jury rendered its verdict, the legislature passed the budget bill, the buzzer ended the basketball game.

It's not that way for a teacher. You still worry, even after you have forgotten their names. You question whether you could have done better. Did they actually learn anything about medieval history? Will the name Charlemagne mean anything? If they ever see a Renaissance painting, will they recall seventh-grade social studies? Will they see themselves as actors in the ongoing drama of human history?

A Teacher's Life

I would be the Plato of Pipkin Middle School. Adoring students would gather at my feet, soaking up wisdom I had gleaned from my years of formal schooling and streetwise journalism. I would pose penetrating questions about truth, justice, and beauty to liberate them from the chains of pop culture inanity and adolescent idiocy, encourage them to escape the shadowy cave of ignorance, and climb toward the sunlight of intellectual illumination.

The Socratic Method would be my pedagogy—ideal for teaching the Middle Ages, whose Scholastic philosophers perfected the "critical-thinking" skills that are prized, but difficult to achieve, by Progressive educational theory. My students would debate the great issues of medieval Europe. They would understand why the Crusades were launched. They would recognize that the much ridiculed dispute, "How many angels can dance on the head of a pin?" was a cerebral exercise over the nature of reality: Are invisible angels, and by analogy concepts like love or honesty, tangible substances? Do they exist in physical space, or are they purely mental abstractions?

At the end of their year with me, students would be adept at forming insightful questions on any topic, able to respond with defensible answers and reject the spurious and absurd—and realize that the ability to do so was a worthy personal achievement.

Well . . . as you have seen, it didn't quite turn out that way. I grossly underestimated the difficulty of persuading fourteen-year-olds that there is a future in studying the past.

While I'm not sure the kids learned much from me, I learned a lot about the malaise pervading too many American schools from them. Most of all, I learned that teaching is not simply lesson plans and textbooks, good intentions and state certification.

Yes, teaching includes lots of questions: "Mr. Awbrey, my dad just got his disability check from the state. What's the best restaurant in town? He wants to treat us." "Mr. Awbrey, I know where to get some good homegrown weed. Want me to get you some?" "Mr. Awbrey, my mom's boyfriend sold my history text to a used book store. Can I get another one?"

Teachers must be many things on any given day—counselor, cop, surrogate parent, advisor to the lovesick, fashion consultant—that have little to do with the state-mandated curriculum but everything to do with establishing the trust that connects them with kids desperately craving, yet often equally desperately resisting, adult direction.

As an opinion writer, I frequently—and, I admit, rather enjoyably—browbeat teachers over what I perceived as their obvious failings and deficiencies. "If the student hasn't learned, the teacher hasn't taught," was my favorite line, one that inevitably drew agreeing nods from most readers and government policy makers.

To all teachers: I apologize.

Coming from journalism, where creativity and individual initiative—spiced with a dash of antiauthoritarian skepticism—are prized traits, I was surprised how little freedom teachers have. Typically isolated in large, impersonal, factorylike buildings, lacking influence over hiring, curriculum, or school routines, subject to decisions by cover-your-ass administrators, the arrogance of smugly complacent bureaucrats, and the taunts of smarty-pants editorial writers, teachers are virtually powerless and daily suffer assaults on their professional dignity. Yet they are supposed to produce students with high academic abilities, good citizenship, and sensitive moral values, who also say no to drugs and alcohol, know how to prevent unwanted pregnancy, and want to save the planet.

Moreover, teachers are asked to form close, meaningful relationships with students, to mold lessons to each individual's learning style and bring out the hidden potential in all children so they can pursue their "passion" in life while also scoring well on state assessment exams. This is to happen in each class of twenty-five to thirty students whose abilities might range from borderline genius to mentally impaired. Only a multitasking Mother Teresa could handle so much, assuming she had a state teacher license and was willing to coach volleyball and police the school lunchroom.

Often treated by their superiors as slightly dense children who can't be trusted with real responsibility, teachers also must suffer a public attitude that sees teaching as a relatively low-skilled career—how hard can it be to work with children?—that anyone with a pulse, a liking for kids, and a college degree could do.

It's not true. But I once believed it.

Ideologues of Education

In June 1989, I visited East Berlin to interview officials of the German Democratic Republic on East-West relations. Comparing the dilapidated, poor, and dull East Berlin to the glittering and wealthy West Berlin a few blocks away, I asked the Communist apparatchiks about the future of their system.

They insisted that the GDR would eventually triumph, arguing that history was on their side and that the Marxist dialectic would prove them right. "Our ideas are indisputably correct," one of them said. "We just have to try harder to make them work."

Six months later, the Berlin Wall crumbled.

Since then, the only people I have encountered as dogmatic about ideas that have clearly failed are members of the U.S. education establishment, notably the professors of education who train the vast majority of the nation's teachers.

Virtually every education school in the country promotes pedagogical concepts developed in the early twentieth century by John Dewey, William Heard Kilpatrick, and other Progressive theorists. Over the past few decades, education professors have imposed an orthodoxy more rigid than that outlined by the original Progressives, as evidenced by their abandonment of Dewey's belief that the liberal arts, especially history and geography, should form the heart of school curricula.

Studies showing that teacher competence is the most important element in student achievement suggest that raising teacher quality should be at the center of school reform. That's why in his education budgets President Barack Obama has earmarked millions of new dollars to improve the nation's teaching force. Much of that money, however, will be wasted unless coupled with a revolution in how the country trains its classroom instructors.

In earlier chapters, I explained my tribulations in education school and classroom misadventures with "project learning," "student-centered instruction," and other Progressive strategies that have caused immense damage to American schooling. In brief, those ordeals undoubtedly cost me some cherished IQ points, confirming educational historian Diane Ravitch's observation that education professors have "numbed the brains of future teachers with endless blather about process and abstract thinking skills."

Just as the hard-line East Germans I met asserted that their system was based on "scientific socialism," American educators maintain that their methodologies are grounded in "sound science"—data-driven, research-based, empirically verified. But a critical reading of education journals usually finds them crammed with recycled Progressive tenets wrapped in trendy social-science terminology.

The result is an unshakeable belief that teaching is principally a technical skill and that—I was repeatedly told by education professors and administrators—"any good teacher can teach any subject." That means education students spend huge amounts of time drafting lesson plans, role-playing as schoolchildren, decorating classrooms, and practicing "sponge" activities to soak up the final few minutes of a class period. Formulas and routines are prized over serious scholarly inquiry and intellectual curiosity.

Teaching majors come from the lowest rungs of the academic ladder. Most bright young people do not want to fritter away priceless and irreplaceable college years on courses short on academic substance and long on party-line indoctrination. Yet many top-notch students from the nation's most respected universities eagerly sign up for such alternative programs as Teach for America that enable them to sidestep education schools to get into the classroom.

What's missing in education schools is the sense that teaching is primarily an art largely dependent on the character, commitment, and intellectual aptitude of the teacher.

Remember your favorite teachers? Most likely they were unique individuals with eccentric teaching styles. They might break the rules, but they had a remarkable ability to capture your attention and interest you in their subject. None were pedagogical clones engineered by education professors to kowtow to school bureaucrats or conform to Progressive ideology.

Toward the end of my entry year at Pipkin Middle School, I realized that I would never fit the Progressive mold. The final blow fell when my principal said that 70 percent of my instructional time the next year must be dedicated to project-method exercises and that I must forsake the "tribal elder at the communal fire" storyteller manner I preferred.

To me, this was a depressing misunderstanding of how people learn history.

Regardless of time period or culture, humans connect with the past mainly through narratives. As a journalist I knew this was true. The finest reporters are usually superb storytellers. But the Progressive canon insists otherwise: arts-and-crafts projects are superior to stories, legends, myths, primary sources, and other literature to commune with the past.

I intentionally missed the deadline to sign my teaching contract for the next year and began work on this book to help Americans better understand the crisis in their schools.

Putting Kids First

Citing a large body of research on child development, Springfield Superintendent Norm Ridder wanted to revamp the district's time schedule so secondary schools started later in the morning and elementary grades began earlier.

Frustrated from facing a roomful of listless, semiconscious adolescents in my 8 a.m. first period, I strongly favored the plan. Most of my students didn't become coherent until midmorning because teenagers run on different circadian rhythms than younger children. A delayed bell would make the older kids more ready to learn.

The proposal set off a firestorm; not among students, who generally liked the idea, but among adults. Bus drivers, cafeteria workers, office staff, and teachers whose personal lives might be inconvenienced by the change howled to the school board, and the scheme was dropped. This in a district that claims to put "children first."

A veteran colleague explained it this way: "You don't understand, David, education is run for the benefit of the adults who work in the schools, not the kids."

That reality means President Barack Obama's main challenge to reform education has come from entrenched adult interests—notably teachers' unions and old-guard Progressive partisans in education schools—certain to resist any program that disturbs the comfort level among school insiders for whom the current system works just fine.

Consider three key elements of the president's education agenda unveiled in early 2010: high academic standards, teacher quality, and expanded charter and other school choice options.

Standards

Ever since I started covering education as a neophyte reporter in the early 1970s, I have suspected that the education establishment would go to astounding lengths to prevent the American people from truly understanding how poorly public schools were educating vast numbers of children.

My suspicion was validated when the 2002 No Child Left Behind law required states to develop tests to assess student performance in math and reading.

Rather than set high proficiency standards, many states drafted exams that any reasonably intelligent golden retriever could easily pass—the better to avoid a public outcry over weak academic skills that might force schools to genuinely reform.

"We've seen a race to the bottom. States are lying to children. They are lying to parents. They're ignoring failure," said U.S. Education Secretary Arne Duncan.

To ensure that all American children have an education suitable for the twenty-first century, the United States needs consistent standards in math, science, and language arts. States and districts would implement their own curricula to meet the benchmarks, but the expectations should be the same in Minnesota as in Mississippi. A start along those lines came in June 2010 when the Common Core State Standards Initiative, backed by the National Governors Association and the Council of Chief School Officers, released plans that could give the country common objectives in math and English.

Once states are measured under the same criteria, the theory goes, the dynamic would switch from dumbing down to smarting up because voters would want their state to be No. 1 and hold governors, school board members, and legislators accountable for student achievement. Maybe.

Teacher Quality

When I was working for the Associated Press in Pennsylvania in the late 1970s, a leader of the state National Education Association said that teachers should stop thinking of themselves as professionals like doctors and lawyers. Instead, he insisted, "Teachers should start acting like steelworkers and make the NEA a real union."

That official got his wish. The NEA and the smaller American Federation of Teachers are among the country's most powerful trade unions. Beholden to the unions' vast sums of campaign cash and their legions of political volunteers, few politicians in Congress or most state legislatures—especially Democrats traditionally supported by unions—have ever defied the unions on any significant issue directly affecting teachers.

The unions, of course, profess a deep devotion to children while demanding rules on tenure, teacher evaluation, salary scales, and other practices that often deny students quality instruction and keep less-than-desirable teachers employed.

One example of many: In Springfield, as in most communities, teachers are assigned to schools based largely on seniority and personal preference. Veteran teachers—supposedly the highest skilled—typically select schools in affluent neighborhoods where students are easier to manage. Rookies go to low-income buildings where they are often overwhelmed by the behavioral and social problems many poor kids bring to class. That leads to a lot of newbie mistakes and high turnover in schools that need experienced, battle-tested teachers.

While unions deserve considerable criticism, it's necessary to note they have scant influence over teacher training, hiring, curriculum, discipline, and other policies. Ideally, teachers would be heavily involved in such classroom matters, but to do so would require teachers to see themselves as accountable professionals rather than rank-and-file laborers.

Choice

Nothing threatens the educational status quo more than permitting parents to choose the school their children attend. Charter schools generally operate outside the union work rules and bureaucratic lethargy typical of many school systems and represent competition that threatens the establishment's monopoly over public schooling. To survive in a choice environment, schools would have to perform to the satisfaction of parents.

In the three elements of his education agenda outlined above, Obama emerges as a sincere school reformer. But his plan faces brutal political opposition. By putting children first, the president can succeed only by upsetting a lot of adults.

The Fragile Line

While in college and trying to impress a girl, a professor, or potential employer with my intellectual prowess, I was a one-trick pony. I would wait for the opportune moment and begin:

Whan that aprill with his shoures soote
The droghte of march hath perced to the roote
And bathed every veyne in swich licour
Of which vertu engendered is the flour.

I am forever grateful to my high school English teacher for requiring us to memorize the first eighteen lines of the prologue to Geoffrey Chaucer's *Canterbury Tales* in the original fourteenth-century Middle English. Following Chaucer's marvelous collection of characters on pilgrimage stimulated my fascination with the medieval era that has never abated.

My experience with Chaucer's poem rebuts arguments that history, literature, and other humanities have no practical or economic merit. While you seldom find help-wanted ads for medieval bards or armored knights in the daily newspaper, nothing has been more valuable to me as a journalist than my liberal arts background. From enhancing critical-reasoning skills by cracking heads with Augustine and Aquinas to understanding politics by analyzing the power struggles between popes and emperors, medieval history has anchored my professional career.

Education today, however, is promoted as a ticket to be punched en route to a well-paying job and its material satisfactions—something that is "useful." I take the classical liberal view that education should also, if not primarily, be about developing oneself as a human being, an heir to cultural achievements as varied as Chinese scroll paintings and American jazz music.

I wanted to pass that heritage on to my seventh graders. To be honest, as a teacher, I disappointed myself. Part of it was my own weaknesses dealing with some exceptionally socially damaged kids. But I also failed because of the severely defective U.S. education system.

The most worrisome thing I learned for American society from teaching at Pipkin and visiting a variety of classrooms in all regions of the country is how vehemently many students dislike school and how few of them are absorbed by academics. Sure, students from affluent and middle-class families are often masters at getting high grades and impressive test scores—"doing school"—to placate parental aspirations that they attend prestigious colleges. But as discussed in such recent books as *The Dumbest Generation* by Mark Bauerlein and *The Age of American Unreason* by Susan Jacoby, a virulent plague of anti-intellectualism pervades American culture and has infected education, perhaps fatally.

"Although people are going to school more and more years, there's no evidence that they know more," Jacoby told the *New York Times*.

Some blame for this trend goes to youthful obsession with television and other technologies marketed primarily for entertainment or socializing. Such pop culture distractions, however, are attractive to kids partly because most American public schools have failed to engage them in authentic learning, to become fully human as defined by centuries of history and philosophy.

Instead of strong curricula and vigorous teaching, U.S. schools are characterized by burdensome certification requirements, pedagogical stupidities, academically deficient teachers, grubbing for tax money while shirking accountability, and educational leaders who blame everyone but themselves for the seemingly inexorable collapse of what was once history's greatest educational system.

Kids intuit that the whole enterprise is a colossal fraud. As long as they keep their heads down, their mouths shut, and master a few basic skills, they know they can float through the entire miserable enterprise with minimal mental exertion. I know. I've been there. I tried to make a difference, only to abandon my hopes in utter frustration, relieved solely by this opportunity to use my journalistic skills to warn the country that, absent root-and-branch reform, U.S. schools will shove the American experiment in democracy into the abyss.

In my most pessimistic moments, I buck up by recalling how Charlemagne rescued Western civilization from barbarism with a fervid belief in the power of education to transform society. I remember that the artists and teachers of the Italian Renaissance remade humanity's image of itself through paint and marble, philosophy and poetry. And from those two examples, I am reassured that Americans today have the same fountains of wisdom—the traditional liberal arts—to inspire our own cultural and intellectual rebirth.

We Americans must chart our own course for schools. But we can learn much from our medieval and Renaissance ancestors: that education is the fragile line between chaos and civilization; that the quest for truth is a primary feature separating humans from beasts; that teachers are midwives to the future; and that what we do today with our schools will largely determine how history remembers our generation of Americans.

~

Acknowledgments

I am deeply grateful to my agent, Robert Astle, for his confidence in this book and his ability to find the best publisher for it. Thanks to Tom Koerner and his staff at Rowman & Littlefield's Education Division for their superb professionalism.

Without the support and love of my wife, Diane Awbrey, this six-year-long teaching and writing experience could never have been completed.

I also want to express affection for my colleagues during my year at Pipkin Middle School, especially fellow members of the seventh-grade Blue Team—Shannon Witherspoon, Hanni Rauch, and Stephanie Beaty—whose help and advice got me through many difficult times. Special appreciation goes Dr. Sharri Harwick, my principal at Pipkin, for her patience and encouragement when I wondered if I could ever survive facing several classrooms full of seventh graders every day.

To my students at Pipkin: I shall never forget you and wish you only the best in life.

~

About the Author

David S. Awbrey has covered education and other public issues in nine states. He was editorial page editor for the largest newspapers in Kansas and Vermont and the leading newspaper in southern Illinois. He was a legislative reporter for United Press International in Maryland, the Associated Press in Pennsylvania, and a statewide newspaper chain in Illinois. He won the 2003 award for best editorial from the Education Writers Association.

In 2004, he left newspaper journalism to become a teacher. He served for six months as communications director of the Kansas State Department of Education to gain an insider's view of school politics and policy making before taking a position teaching social studies at Pipkin Middle School in Springfield, Missouri.

Awbrey holds a bachelor's degree in history, with a concentration on the Middle Ages, and a master's in religious studies, with a focus on the medieval and Renaissance/Reformation periods, from the University of Kansas. He was a National Endowment for the Humanities professional journalism fellow at Stanford University. He has taught journalism courses at Southern Illinois University-Carbondale and the University of Kansas.

His book, *Finding Hope in the Age of Melancholy*, a memoir of midlife depression and recovery, was published in 1999 by Little, Brown and Company.

He lives in Springfield with his wife and daughter.

CPSIA information can be obtained at www.ICGtesting.com
Printed in the USA
BVOW040445071211

277669BV00002B/1/P